BOOSTING YOUR ENGLISH VOCABULARY

DR. GOVIND PRASAD GOYAL, MR. SRIKANTA M
MR. SRIKANTA M

DEDICATED

To

ALL KEEN LEARNERS OF ENGLISH

Contents

Foreword

"Boosting Your English Vocabulary" is a comprehensive guide to improving your English vocabulary and mastering powerful expressions. This book is an essential resource for anyone looking to enhance their language skills.

The book is divided into several chapters, each focusing on a different aspect of vocabulary building. One of the unique features of this book is its emphasis on practical application. Each chapter includes numerous examples of how to use vocabulary in real-life situations, making it easier for readers to understand and remember the words and expressions. The book also includes exercises and quizzes to test your understanding and reinforce your learning.

The writing style is clear, concise, and engaging, making the book accessible to readers of all levels. He draws on his extensive experience as an educator to provide practical tips and insights that are sure to benefit anyone looking to improve their English vocabulary.

Overall, "Boosting Your English Vocabulary" is an excellent resource for anyone looking to enhance their language skills. Whether you are a student, a professional, or simply someone looking to improve your communication skills, this book is sure to provide you with the tools and knowledge you need to succeed.

Dr. Ajay Kumar Gupta
Dean-Academics, IMS-Noida &
Former Director- IT
University of Delhi

Preface

Welcome to "Boosting your English Vocabulary"! In this book, we embark on a journey to enhance your command over the English language by expanding your vocabulary. Whether you are a student, a professional, or simply someone who wants to express themselves more eloquently, this book is designed to help you achieve your goals.

The ability to communicate effectively in English is a valuable skill in today's globalized world. It opens doors to countless opportunities, whether in academia, career advancement, or personal relationships. However, building a strong vocabulary is no easy task. It requires time, effort, and, most importantly, practice.

In this book, we take a practical approach to vocabulary building. We understand that memorizing long lists of words can be tedious and ineffective. Instead, we focus on providing you with the tools and strategies to actively engage with new words and incorporate them into your everyday speech and writing.

Throughout the chapters, you will find a variety of exercises, activities, and examples that encourage you to interact with the English language in meaningful ways. We believe that learning should be enjoyable, and so we have incorporated fun and engaging exercises that will keep you motivated on your vocabulary-building journey.

Expressions are an essential part of any language, adding depth, nuance, and authenticity to your communication. In this book, we not only introduce you to new words but also explore how to use them in practice. You will discover common idiomatic expressions, phrasal verbs, collocations, and more. By understanding and using these expressions, you will be able to convey your thoughts and ideas with greater precision and fluency.

Remember, building a strong vocabulary is a continuous process. It requires regular practice and exposure to new words. This book serves as a starting point, providing you with a solid foundation to expand upon. As you progress through the chapters, we encourage you to actively engage with the material, experiment with new words and expressions, and seek opportunities to use them in your daily life.

Ultimately, our goal is to help you boost your English vocabulary and empower you to communicate effectively in any situation. So, without further ado, let's embark on this exciting journey together and unlock the power of words!

Happy learning,

Authors

Acknowledgements

We extend our heartfelt gratitude to everyone who contributed to the creation of Boosting Your English Vocabulary. Your support, guidance, and encouragement have been invaluable throughout this journey.

Our deepest thanks go to our mentors whose passion for teaching has inspired us every step of the way. Your insightful feedback and unwavering guidance have played a pivotal role in shaping this book.

We are immensely grateful to our friends and family for their constant support and belief in our abilities. Your encouragement gave us the strength to overcome challenges and strive for excellence.

Special appreciation goes to the editors and proofreaders who meticulously reviewed and refined the manuscript. Your attention to detail and commitment to quality have enhanced the clarity and coherence of this book.

We also acknowledge the invaluable insights and expertise of English language teachers and educators, whose dedication to language proficiency and vocabulary enrichment has greatly influenced this work.

Finally, our deepest gratitude goes to the readers of this book. Your enthusiasm for learning and improving your English vocabulary has motivated us to create a resource that meets your needs. We hope this book significantly contributes to your language journey.

To all who played a part, however big or small, in the development and publication of Boosting Your English Vocabulary, we sincerely thank you.

Dr. Govind Prasad Goyal
Associate Professor (English)
IMS Law College, Noida
&
Srikanta M
Assistant Professor,
Department of English,
Division of Languages,
Department of Health System Management Studies,
School of Life Sciences,
JSS Academy of Higher Education & Research,
Mysuru, Karnataka, India

Prologue

In the labyrinth of words and ideas, the art of communication reigns supreme. Language, the foundation of our interactions, serves as the bridge that connects us, transcending borders and cultures. Within the vast expanse of the English language lies a world of possibilities, where the strength of one's vocabulary determines the depth and breadth of their expression.

"Boosting Your English Vocabulary" is an expedition into the realm of words, designed to empower and elevate your linguistic prowess. It is a guidebook crafted with passion and precision, tailored to sharpen your linguistic acumen and unravel the enigma of language.

Within these pages, we embark on a transformative journey, a voyage that transcends mere memorization and rote learning. Here, we delve into the realm of powerful expressions, where words become an artist's brush and sentences transform into poetic tapestries. Through careful exploration and practice, we unlock the secrets of language, unearthing the hidden treasures buried within the lexicon.

Each chapter serves as a gateway to a multitude of words, expressions, and idioms, carefully curated to enrich your vocabulary and amplify your communication skills. The power of metaphor, the elegance of alliteration, and the rhythm of figurative language dance across the pages, inviting you to join in the linguistic symphony.

As you journey through the chapters, you will witness the metamorphosis of words into living entities, infused with meaning and intention. Engage in exercises that challenge your creative faculties, encouraging you to craft vivid descriptions, construct persuasive arguments, and immerse yourself in the vivid tapestry of language.

But this book is more than a mere collection of words and expressions. It is a testament to the power of language itself—the power to inspire, to connect, and to transform. Through its teachings, you will unlock new doors of opportunity, gaining the ability to captivate minds, influence hearts, and leave an indelible mark on those you encounter.

So, Dear reader, let us embark on this linguistic odyssey together, where each word is a stepping stone, and each expression a beacon guiding us to new horizons. By embracing the art of vocabulary enrichment, you hold within your hands the key to unlocking the true potential of language and opening doors to a world of endless possibilities.

CHAPTER ONE

The Power of Words: Unlocking Your Vocabulary Potential

Words have an incredible power to shape our thoughts, influence others, and transform our lives. By expanding your vocabulary, you unlock a vast arsenal of linguistic tools that can elevate your communication to new heights. In this chapter, we will explore the profound impact of words and provide examples of how powerful expressions are used by intelligent debaters, inspiring commencement speakers, BBC news readers, orators, politicians, and others.

Words have the ability to inspire, motivate, and incite action. Consider the famous words of Martin Luther King Jr., "*I have a dream.*" These simple yet profound words became a rallying cry for the civil rights movement, igniting passion and fueling the quest for equality. King's eloquence and use of powerful expressions touched the hearts of millions, demonstrating the transformative power of words.

In the realm of debating, intelligence-squared debaters employ a range of expressions to make their arguments more persuasive. They skillfully utilize rhetorical devices such as metaphors, analogies, and similes to bring their points to life. For instance, when discussing the importance of education, a debater might say, "*Education is the key that unlocks the doors of opportunity.*" This vivid metaphor paints a vivid picture in the minds of the audience, emphasizing the transformative potential of education.

Commencement speakers are known for their ability to captivate and inspire graduates. They often employ powerful expressions to convey life lessons and motivate individuals to pursue their dreams. For example, in his commencement address at Stanford University, Steve Jobs famously said, "*Your time is limited, don't waste it living someone else's life.*" This succinct yet impactful statement encourages graduates to embrace their individuality and seize the opportunities that come their way.

During NYU's 2022 Commencement, address, the host addressed the crowd by introducing Taylor Swift with the following expressions:

Taylor, you are a role model across the world for your unprecedented talent and accomplishment,

-a blazing singer, songwriter, producer, director, actress, pioneering and influential advocate for artists' rights, and philanthropist. You have brought joy and resolve to your hundreds of millions of fans throughout the world.

When it comes to news reading, BBC presenters masterfully employ a range of vocabulary to convey information with authority and credibility. Their use of precise language helps clarify complex concepts for the audience. For instance, when reporting on economic downturns, a news reader might say, "*The economy is teetering on the brink of recession.*" This expression creates a sense of urgency and emphasizes the gravity of the situation, effectively conveying the state of the economy to the viewers.

Orators and public speakers understand the importance of captivating an audience through their words. They utilize rhetorical devices such as alliteration, repetition, and parallelism to enhance the impact of their message. Consider the famous words of Winston Churchill during World War II: "*We shall fight on the beaches, we shall fight on the landing grounds, we shall fight in the fields and in the streets.*" The use of repetition and parallel structure in this speech instilled a sense of determination and unity among the British people, inspiring them to persevere in the face of adversity.

Politicians, too, harness the power of words to sway public opinion and rally support for their causes. They employ persuasive language, emotional appeals, and powerful expressions to connect with voters. Former US

President Barack Obama's campaign slogan, *"Yes, we can,"* resonated with millions of people and became a symbol of hope and unity.

The examples mentioned here only scratch the surface of the countless ways powerful expressions are used by influential figures. By consciously expanding your vocabulary and incorporating these expressions into your own communication, you can unlock your full potential as a speaker, writer, and thinker. Embrace the art of storytelling, master the techniques of persuasion, and strive for clarity and precision in your words.

Ultimately, the power of words lies in their ability to shape perceptions, evoke emotions, and drive change. By unlocking your vocabulary potential and harnessing the power of expressions used by intelligent debaters, inspiring commencement speakers, BBC news readers, orators, politicians, and others, you can become a more impactful communicator. Your words have the potential to inspire, motivate, and transform lives. So, embrace the journey of expanding your vocabulary and discovering the true power of words.

Exercises

Exploring the power of words is a fantastic way to unlock your vocabulary potential. Here are a few engaging exercises to get started:

Exercise 1: Word Map

Objective: Expand your vocabulary by associating new words with familiar ones.

Instructions:

1. Choose a central word (e.g., "communication").
2. Draw a map connecting this word to related terms (e.g., "dialogue," "expression," "articulation").
3. For each related term, create another level of connections with synonyms and related concepts.
4. Write sentences using the new words.

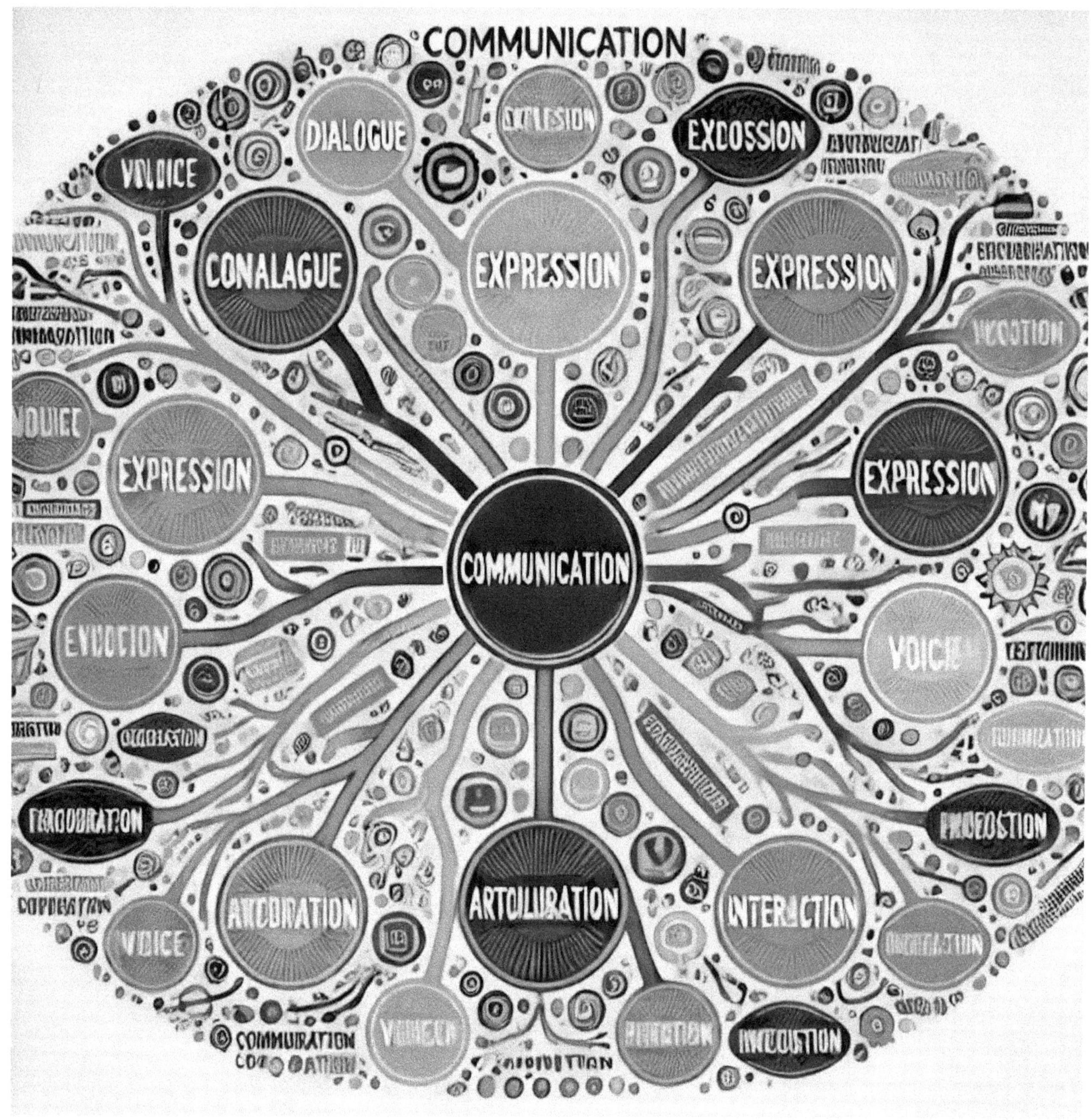

Mindmap on Communication

Exercise 2: Word Journal
Objective: Track and use new words daily.
Instructions:

1. Keep a small notebook with you.
2. Write down any new or interesting words you come across.
3. Include the definition, example sentences, and your own sentence using the word.
4. Review your journal weekly and try to use these words in conversations.

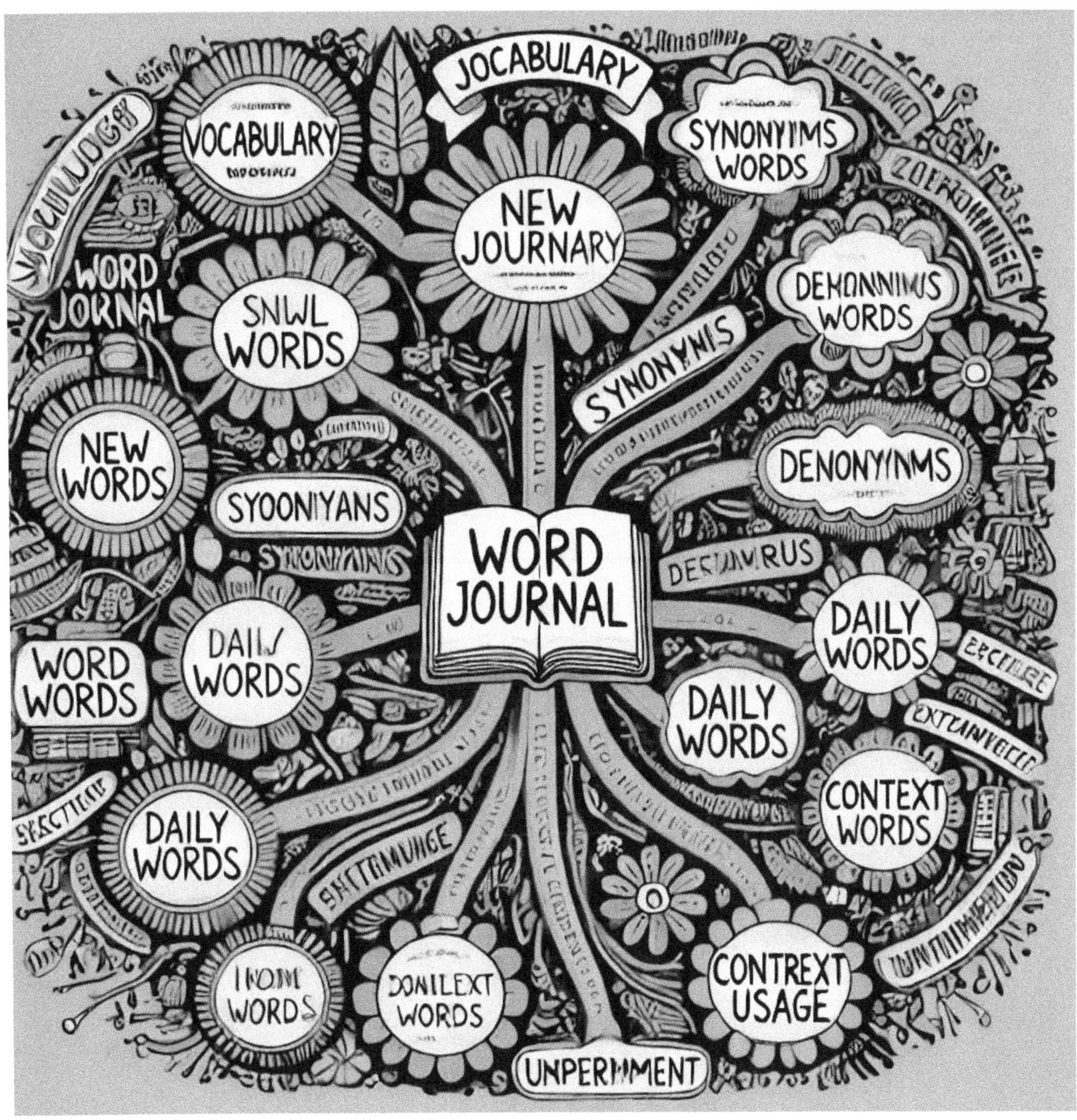

Word Journal

Exercise 3: Synonym Challenge
Objective: Improve your ability to find synonyms and use them in context.
Instructions:

1. Take a common word (e.g., "happy").
2. List as many synonyms as you can (e.g., "joyful," "cheerful," "ecstatic").
3. Write a short story or paragraph using **as many of these synonyms as possible.**

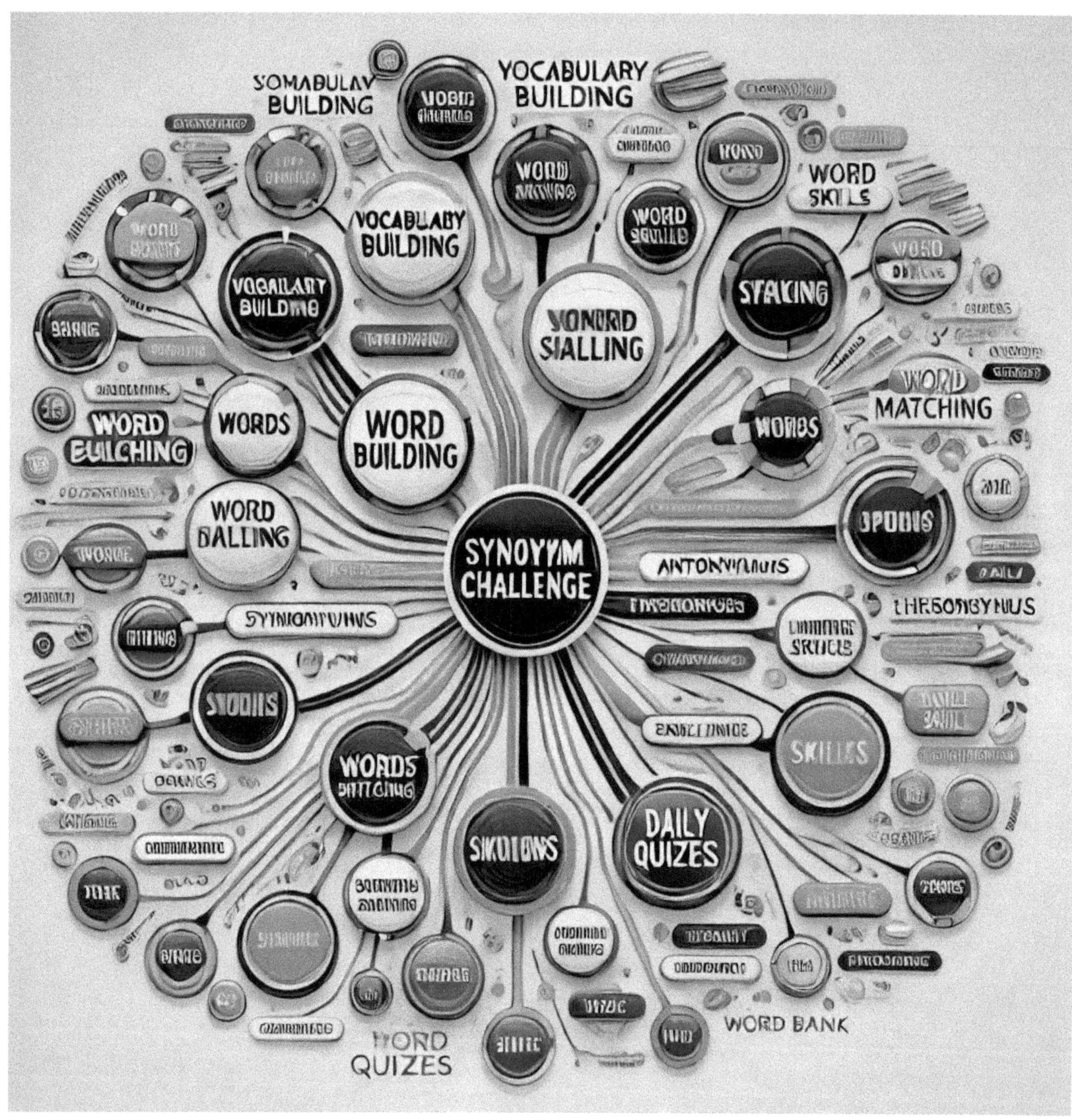

Synonym Challenge

Exercise 4: Word Transformation
Objective: Practice transforming words to fit different grammatical contexts.
Instructions:

1. Select a root word (e.g., "beauty").
2. Transform it into different forms: adjective (beautiful), verb (beautify), adverb (beautifully).
3. Create sentences with each form of the word.

Let us select a root word:
Example: "beauty"
Transform it into different forms:
Adjective: beautiful
Verb: beautify
Adverb: beautifully
Create sentences with each form of the word:
Root Word (Noun):
"The beauty of the sunset left everyone speechless."
Adjective:
"The beautiful flowers in the garden attracted many visitors."
Verb:
"She decided to beautify her home with new furniture and decorations."
Adverb:
"He painted the portrait beautifully, capturing every detail with precision."
Expanded Exercise: Additional Words
Select another root word:
Example: "strength"
Transform it into different forms:
Adjective: strong
Verb: strengthen
Adverb: strongly
Create sentences with each form of the word:
Root Word (Noun):
"His strength was unparalleled in the competition."
Adjective:
"She is a strong advocate for environmental conservation."
Verb:
"Daily exercises will strengthen your muscles."
Adverb:
"He felt strongly about the importance of education."
Additional Tips:
Practice with a variety of root words to enhance your vocabulary and understanding of word transformations.

Challenge yourself to use the transformed words in different contexts, such as writing essays, stories, or even casual conversations.

Review and expand your word list regularly to ensure continuous growth in your vocabulary skills.

I hope these exercises help you unlock your vocabulary potential and appreciate the power of words even more!

Exercise 5: Vocabulary Building Games
Objective: Make vocabulary building fun and interactive.
Instructions:

1. Play word games like Scrabble, Boggle, or Wordscapes.
2. Use online platforms likeVocabulary.comor Quizlet to engage in vocabulary quizzes and games.
3. Challenge friends or family to a word game competition.

Play Word Games:
Scrabble: This classic board game challenges you to create words from a set of letter tiles. It's a great way to learn new words and practice spelling.

Boggle: In this game, you shake a grid of lettered dice to form words within a time limit. The more words you find, the more points you score.

Wordscapes: This mobile app combines crossword puzzles with word search. It's a relaxing way to enhance your vocabulary on the go.

Wordle: This popular online game gives you six attempts to guess a five-letter word. It's a quick and engaging way to boost your word skills.

Use Online Platforms:
Vocabulary.com: This website offers personalized vocabulary lists and quizzes to help you learn new words and track your progress.

Quizlet: Create your own flashcards or use pre-made sets to study new words and their meanings. You can also play various games to reinforce your learning.

Merriam-Webster: The website offers a "Word of the Day" feature and various word games to challenge your vocabulary skills.

Challenge Friends or Family:
Word Game Competitions: Organize friendly competitions with friends or family members. Set a time limit and see who can come up with the most words or score the highest points.

Spelling Bees: Hold a spelling bee to test each other's spelling skills. It's a fun way to learn new words and improve your spelling accuracy.

Word Puzzles: Solve crossword puzzles or anagrams together. Working as a team can make vocabulary building a fun and social activity.

Additional Tips:
Mix It Up: Combine different games and activities to keep things interesting and prevent monotony.

Set Goals: Aim to learn a certain number of new words each week. Track your progress and celebrate your achievements.

Stay Consistent: Make vocabulary building a regular part of your routine. Even a few minutes each day can make a big difference over time.

By incorporating these engaging activities into your routine, you'll find that vocabulary building becomes an enjoyable and rewarding experience. Happy word hunting!

Exercise 6: Contextual Learning

Objective: Understand and remember new words by learning them in context.

Instructions:

Engage with Varied Content:

Read Books: Choose genres that interest you, whether it's fiction, non-fiction, or specialized fields. Pay attention to how new vocabulary is used within sentences.

Example: "Pride and Prejudice" by Jane Austen is a great book for understanding rich English vocabulary and societal terms.

Read Articles and Journals: Explore magazines, scientific journals, and online articles. They often use domain-specific vocabulary that can expand your word bank.

Example: Reading articles on National Geographic or Scientific American for science-related terms.

Watch Shows and Movies:

Choose Varied Genres: Watch documentaries, dramas, comedies, and educational programs. Observe how different contexts influence word usage.

Example: Watching "The Crown" can help you learn historical and formal vocabulary.

Use Subtitles: Turn on subtitles to see the words as they're spoken. This can improve your understanding and retention.

Example: Watching "Friends" with English subtitles to catch idiomatic expressions.

Listen to Podcasts and Audiobooks:

Find Engaging Topics: Pick podcasts and audiobooks that interest you. This auditory learning helps reinforce new vocabulary through repetition and context.

Example: Listening to the "TED Talks Daily" podcast to hear advanced vocabulary used in various topics.

Take Notes: Write down new words you hear and look up their meanings. Try using them in your own sentences.

Example: Listening to "The Alchemist" by Paulo Coelho as an audiobook and noting down impactful phrases.

Keep a Contextual Vocabulary Journal:

Record New Words: Whenever you come across a new word, jot it down in your journal along with its context.

Example Entry:

Word: Altruistic

Context: "His altruistic actions during the crisis were commendable."

Meaning: Showing selfless concern for the well-being of others.

Practice Sentences: Write your own sentences using the new word to reinforce learning.

Discuss and Use New Words:

Conversations: Make a conscious effort to use new words in your conversations. Discussing topics with friends or colleagues can help embed the words in your memory.

Example: Use new vocabulary words in discussions about a recent book or movie you watched.

Writing: Incorporate new words into your writing, whether it's emails, essays, or creative writing.

Example: Write a short story or a blog post using some of the new words you've learned.

Additional Tips:

Repeat and Reinforce: Repetition is key to memory. Regularly review your vocabulary journal and use new words in different contexts.

Stay Curious: Always be on the lookout for new words and their meanings. Curiosity will naturally enhance your vocabulary.

Make Connections: Relate new words to words you already know. This can help you understand and remember them better.

By engaging with content and learning words in context, you'll find that your vocabulary grows more naturally and effectively. Enjoy the process of discovering the nuances and beauty of language!

Exercise 7: Word of the Day

Objective: Introduce and reinforce new vocabulary daily.

Instructions:

Subscribe to a "Word of the Day" Service:

Websites and Apps: Many websites and apps offer daily vocabulary words. Some popular choices include Merriam-Webster, Dictionary.com, andVocabulary.com.

Email Subscriptions: Sign up for daily word emails from your favorite dictionary or vocabulary-building website.

Apps: Download apps like Word of the Day, Vocabulary Builder, or Quizlet to receive daily notifications.

Write the Word, Its Definition, and an Example Sentence on a Sticky Note:

Step-by-Step:

Choose a Word: Each day, pick the new word provided by your chosen service.

Write the Definition: Ensure you understand the meaning of the word.

Example Sentence: Create or note down an example sentence that uses the word in context.

Sticky Note: Write the word, definition, and example sentence on a sticky note.

Place the Sticky Note Somewhere Visible and Try to Use the Word Throughout the Day:

Visible Locations: Place the sticky note on your desk, computer monitor, refrigerator, or any place you frequently look at.

Use the Word: Make a conscious effort to use the word in your conversations, writing, or thinking process during the day.

Expanded Instructions:

Create a "Word Wall":

Collect Sticky Notes: As you accumulate more words, start placing the sticky notes on a designated wall or board.

Review Regularly: Glance at your word wall daily to reinforce your memory of previously learned words.

Organize by Category: Group words by themes, such as emotions, actions, or descriptions, to better understand their usage.

Daily Word Challenges:

Set Goals: Challenge yourself to use the word of the day a specific number of times in conversations or writing.

Track Usage: Keep a tally of how many times you use the word. Aim to increase this number over time.

Reflection: At the end of the day, reflect on how you used the word and think of additional sentences where it can fit.

Engage in Creative Writing:

Short Stories: Write a short story or a paragraph that includes the word of the day. This helps in understanding the word in various contexts.

Journal Entries: Incorporate the word into your daily journal entries. This practice can make the new vocabulary part of your natural writing style.

Share with Friends or Family:

Word Exchanges: Share your word of the day with friends or family members. Encourage them to do the same.

Joint Learning: Discuss how you each used the word in sentences or daily activities. This can enhance mutual learning and make the process more enjoyable.

Review and Test Yourself:

Weekly Review: At the end of each week, review all the words you've learned. Test yourself on their meanings and usage.

Quizzes: Create or find quizzes that test your knowledge of the words you've learned. This can help reinforce your memory and identify areas for improvement.

By making the "Word of the Day" exercise a part of your daily routine and expanding on it with these additional activities, you'll steadily build and reinforce a robust vocabulary. Enjoy the process of learning new words and watching your language skills flourish!

These exercises should help you tap into the full potential of your vocabulary. Enjoy the journey of exploring the world of words!

CHAPTER TWO

The Art of Persuasion: Enhancing Your Rhetorical Skills

Throughout history, the ability to persuade and influence others has been a highly demanding skill. From ancient philosophers and orators to modern politicians and business leaders, the art of persuasion has played a vital role in shaping opinions, mobilizing crowds, and driving change. Rhetoric, the art of effective communication and persuasion, has been studied and practiced for centuries, honing the skills necessary to influence the human mind.

This chapter delves into the intricacies of persuasion and explores basic principles and techniques for improving public speaking skills. Understanding the art of persuasion can help you communicate more persuasively in personal relationships, work, and public speaking. From mastering the power of language and framing arguments to building credibility and dealing with emotions, we explore the key ingredients needed for persuasive communication.

Power of language

Language is a primary tool of persuasion, and mastering its nuances is essential to effective communication. Your choice of words, tone, and style can greatly affect the impact of your message. This section explores different language techniques to improve your persuasion skills. Clarity and simplicity:

- The importance of clear and concise language.
- Avoid jargon and jargon.
- Simplify complex ideas for better understanding.
- Living images and metaphors:
- Creating mental images using living language.
- Use metaphors to make abstract concepts easier to understand. Use the power of storytelling to engage your audience.

Rhythm and repetition:

- Use rhythm and repetition to emphasize and remember.
- The art of writing catchy slogans and catchphrases.
- The Role of Rhythm and Tempo in Persuasive SpeechPersuasive Argument Structure

Argument structure forms the backbone of persuasive communication. In this section, we'll look at the key elements of a persuasive argument and how to place them effectively.

Introduction and Featured Opening:

- It's important to grab your audience's attention right from the start.

- Use compelling anecdotes, interesting facts, or thought-provoking questions.

Establish credibility:

We build trust and credibility through our expertise, experience, and shared values.

- Use evidence, statistics, and testimonials to support your claims.
- An Appeal to Logical Thinking and Reason:
- Present a logical set of ideas and arguments.
- Using deductive and inductive reasoning.
- Anticipate objections and handle them effectively.

Emotional Appeal:

- Recognize the power of emotions to influence decision-making. It appeals to empathy, compassion, and shared values.
- Use storytelling and personal anecdotes to create emotional connections.

Call to action:

- Encourage your audience to take a certain action or have a certain point of view.
- Provide clear and actionable instructions.
- Create a sense of urgency and importance.

Nonverbal Communication and Body Language

Words are very important, but nonverbal communication and body language also play an important role in persuasion. This section examines the impact of nonverbal cues and how to use them effectively.

- Eye contact and facial expressions:
- Build trust and connection through eye contact.

Use facial expressions to express sincerity, excitement, or concern. Gestures and Postures:

- Use targeted gestures to emphasize your message.
- Maintain an open and confident demeanor to convey credibility.

Vocal modulation and tone:

- Use changes in pitch, volume, and tone to convey emotion.
- Importance of clarity and articulation of voice.

Build relationships and customize your message :

Connecting with your audience on a personal level is critical to effective persuasion. This section provides strategies for building relationships and tailoring your message to different individuals and groups.

Target group analysis:

- Understand the demographics, values and beliefs of your target audience.
- Adjust your wording, examples, and arguments to their point of view.

Establish common ground:

Find common values and experiences to create a sense of unity. Emphasize mutual benefits and common goals.
Active listening and empathy:

- The importance of listening carefully to understand your audience's concerns.
- Show empathy and respond to emotional needs.

Ethical Considerations:

- Persuasion without manipulation or coercion.
- Ensure transparency and honesty in your communications. V. Practice, Feedback, Continuous Improvement (Word)

Exercise 1: Analyzing Rhetorical Devices

Objective: Identify and understand the use of rhetorical devices in famous speeches. Instructions:

Choose a Speech: Select a famous speech, such as Martin Luther King Jr.'s "I Have a Dream" or Winston Churchill's "We Shall Fight on the Beaches."

Identify Rhetorical Devices: Look for examples of rhetorical devices such as ethos, pathos, logos, repetition, metaphors, and analogies.

Analyze Effectiveness: Analyze how these devices contribute to the persuasiveness of the speech. Write a short essay discussing your findings.

Exercise 2: Imitation Exercise

Objective: Practice delivering a speech using the same rhetorical techniques as a famous speaker. Instructions:

Choose a Passage: Select a passage from a famous speech.

Imitate the Style: Write your own speech on a different topic, imitating the rhetorical style and techniques used in the chosen passage.

Deliver the Speech: Practice delivering your speech with the same passion and conviction as the original speaker.

Exercise 3: Persuasive Argument Creation

Objective: Create a persuasive argument using rhetorical techniques. Instructions:

Select a Topic: Choose a topic you are passionate about.

Use Rhetorical Devices: Write a persuasive argument incorporating rhetorical devices such as ethos, pathos, and logos.

Refine and Practice: Refine your argument and practice delivering it with confidence and clarity.

Exercise 4: Speech Reconstruction

Objective: Understand the structure and flow of persuasive speeches. Instructions:

Choose a Speech: Select a famous speech and break it down into its key components (introduction, main points, conclusion).

Reconstruct the Speech: Rewrite the speech in your own words, maintaining the original structure and flow.

Present the Speech: Practice delivering the reconstructed speech.

Exercise 5: Audience Adaptation

Objective: Tailor your persuasive message to different audiences. Instructions:

Choose a Speech: Select a persuasive speech and analyze the intended audience.

Modify for Different Audiences: Rewrite the speech for different audiences (e.g., a younger audience, a professional audience, a skeptical audience).

Compare and Contrast: Compare the different versions of the speech and discuss how the language and rhetorical techniques change based on the audience.

Exercise 6: Emotional Appeal

Objective: Enhance your ability to appeal to the emotions of your audience. Instructions:

Select a Topic: Choose an emotional topic, such as a personal story or a social issue.

Use Pathos: Write a speech that primarily uses emotional appeals (pathos) to persuade the audience.

Deliver with Emotion: Practice delivering the speech with appropriate tone, facial expressions, and body language to convey emotion effectively.

Exercise 7: Persuasive Storytelling

Objective: Use storytelling to enhance your persuasive message. Instructions:

Choose a Story: Select a relevant story that supports your persuasive message.

Incorporate Rhetorical Devices: Integrate rhetorical devices such as imagery, repetition, and anecdotes into the storytelling.

Connect to the Message: Ensure the story clearly connects to your overall persuasive message and reinforces your argument.

Here is a persuasive story that highlights the power of determination and the importance of following one's dreams:

Title: The Dream Weaver

In a small, bustling town lived a young girl named Maya. She was an imaginative soul, always dreaming of creating beautiful art that would inspire others. Her room was filled with sketches, paintings, and sculptures, each piece reflecting her vibrant spirit and boundless creativity.

Despite her passion, Maya faced many challenges. Her family, though loving, struggled to make ends meet. Her father worked long hours in a factory, and her mother took up odd jobs to support the family. They encouraged Maya to focus on practical skills that could guarantee a stable income, rather than pursuing her artistic dreams.

But Maya's heart was set on attending the prestigious Art Institute in the city. She believed that if she could get the right training, she could become a renowned artist and bring joy to countless people through her work. Determined to follow her dream, Maya decided to take a leap of faith.

To raise money for her tuition, Maya started offering art lessons to children in her neighborhood. She also took on commissions, painting murals and portraits for local businesses and families. Her dedication paid off, and soon she had saved enough to apply to the Art Institute.

The day of her interview arrived, and Maya was filled with a mix of excitement and nerves. She presented her portfolio, showcasing her best pieces, and spoke passionately about her vision for the future. The admissions committee was impressed by her talent and determination. Maya was granted a scholarship, which covered most of her tuition fees.

At the Art Institute, Maya flourished. She learned new techniques, experimented with different mediums, and collaborated with other talented artists. Her work began to gain recognition, and she was invited to exhibit her pieces in various galleries.

Years later, Maya's dream had come true. She had become a celebrated artist, known for her unique style and ability to evoke powerful emotions through her art. Her pieces were displayed in renowned museums, and she was invited to give talks and workshops around the world.

Maya's journey was a testament to the power of determination and the importance of following one's dreams. She proved that with hard work, perseverance, and a belief in oneself, even the most challenging obstacles can be overcome.

Moral of the Story: Maya's story reminds us that dreams are worth pursuing, no matter the challenges. It encourages us to stay true to our passions and believe in our abilities. By following our dreams with determination and resilience, we can create a brighter and more fulfilling future for ourselves and inspire others along the way.

Additional Tips:

- Study Famous Speeches: Regularly read or watch famous speeches to learn from master orators.
- Practice Regularly: Consistent practice is key to improving your rhetorical skills.
- Seek Feedback: Ask for feedback from peers, mentors, or coaches to refine your persuasive techniques.

By practicing these exercises and incorporating rhetorical techniques from famous speeches, you'll enhance your ability to persuade and engage any audience. Enjoy the journey of mastering the art of persuasion!

CHAPTER THREE

Language as a Weapon: Harnessing the Power of Debating Expressions

Language is one of humanity's most potent tools, and the English language, with its vast lexicon and global reach, holds a special place in the realms of communication, diplomacy, and debate. It has often been said that words are mightier than the sword, and when used strategically, they can influence, persuade, and even change the course of history. In the context of debating, the English language becomes a weapon—albeit a peaceful one—that shapes ideas, shifts perceptions, and facilitates discourse. Debaters, by mastering its nuances, wield this tool to craft compelling arguments, dismantle opposing views, and ultimately sway audiences. This essay explores the many ways in which English serves as a weapon in debates, through persuasive expressions, rhetorical strategies, and powerful examples from history.

The Art of Persuasion through Language

At the core of any debate is the art of persuasion. English, with its rich diversity of expressions and idioms, provides debaters with a range of linguistic tools to persuade effectively. A well-articulated argument doesn't just present facts; it frames them in ways that appeal to logic, emotion, and credibility—what Aristotle referred to as logos, pathos, and ethos.

For instance, when a debater appeals to logos, they use rational and logical expressions that enhance their argument's credibility. Words like "therefore," "hence," and "consequently" are connectors that lead the audience down a path of logical reasoning. Consider a debater arguing in favor of climate change action: "The evidence from the Intergovernmental Panel on Climate Change (IPCC) reports clearly indicates that global temperatures are rising due to human activities. Hence, if we do not reduce emissions now, we are bound to face catastrophic consequences in the near future." The use of "hence" in this context strengthens the cause-and-effect relationship, driving home the need for action.

On the other hand, pathos plays to the emotions of the audience. Debaters often use emotionally charged words or vivid descriptions to elicit empathy or urgency. Consider Martin Luther King Jr.'s "I Have a Dream" speech, a masterclass in emotional appeal, where he used the English language to unite millions by evoking the pain and suffering of racial segregation while painting a hopeful picture of equality. In debates, similar strategies can sway an audience. A debater arguing against war might say, "War is not just numbers on a battlefield—it is fathers torn from children, cities reduced to rubble, and dreams forever shattered." The emotive language here humanizes the subject, engaging the audience's empathy.

Finally, ethos refers to the speaker's credibility and trustworthiness. Language plays a pivotal role in establishing ethos by demonstrating the speaker's knowledge, character, and respect. For example, a debater might use expressions such as "As a scholar in this field," or "Based on extensive research," to reinforce their authority. Even subtler linguistic choices, such as a respectful tone or acknowledging opposing viewpoints graciously, can build credibility. A classic example is Barack Obama's speeches, where he often began by acknowledging the complexities of issues and the legitimacy of opposing viewpoints, thus fostering trust before presenting his stance.

Rhetorical Devices in Debate

Beyond basic persuasive strategies, English offers a treasure trove of rhetorical devices that debaters use to sharpen their arguments. Techniques such as repetition, metaphors, analogies, and antithesis help debaters make their points more memorable and impactful.

Repetition is a powerful way to hammer home a key point. In debate, when a phrase or idea is repeated, it not only emphasizes its importance but also makes it more likely to stick in the audience's mind. Consider Winston Churchill's famous speech during World War II, where he declared, "We shall fight on the beaches, we shall fight on the landing grounds, we shall fight in the fields and in the streets, we shall fight in the hills; we shall never surrender." The repeated phrase "we shall fight" stirs determination and solidarity, demonstrating the power of repetition in speech.

Metaphors and analogies are other linguistic weapons in debate. By comparing complex ideas to familiar concepts, debaters can make abstract or technical issues more relatable. For instance, in a debate about data privacy, a speaker might say, "Allowing companies to track your online behavior without consent is like leaving your front door wide open—anyone can walk in and take what they want." This analogy simplifies a complex issue and makes it easier for the audience to grasp the dangers of privacy invasion.

Similarly, antithesis—the juxtaposition of opposing ideas—can create striking contrasts that highlight the stakes of a debate. A debater might say, "We can either stand by and do nothing as the planet burns, or we can act now and preserve a livable world for future generations." The stark contrast between "stand by" and "act now" underlines the urgency of the issue, leaving little room for neutral ground.

Historical Examples of English as a Debating Weapon

Throughout history, the English language has been used as a tool for debate and persuasion by some of the most influential figures. Abraham Lincoln, one of the greatest orators in American history, demonstrated how language could be used to unite a divided nation. His Gettysburg Address is a testament to the power of succinct, poignant language. At just over two minutes long, the speech used phrases such as "government of the people, by the people, for the people" to rally support for the Union and redefine the American identity. The clarity and brevity of his words made his message accessible to all, ensuring its lasting impact.

Another historical example is Margaret Thatcher's use of language in her debates and speeches. Known as the "Iron Lady," Thatcher was renowned for her sharp, no-nonsense style, using precise language to convey strength and resolve. In debates, she often employed rhetorical questions to challenge her opponents and force them to confront uncomfortable truths. In a famous exchange with Labour leader Neil Kinnock, she asked, "Why does he keep referring to what's happening in the future? Why doesn't he give some figures from the past?" Her pointed question deflected the argument back to Kinnock, highlighting inconsistencies in his position.

More recently, figures like Malala Yousafzai have shown how English can be used as a weapon in debates about human rights. Addressing the United Nations, Malala's speech on girls' education used simple yet powerful language: "One child, one teacher, one book, one pen can change the world." Her choice of words underscored the profound impact of education, while the repetition of "one" emphasized the individual's power to make a difference.

To conclude, the English language, with its vast array of expressions, rhetorical devices, and historical legacy, serves as a powerful weapon in debate. Whether through logical arguments, emotional appeals, or the establishment of credibility, debaters use the nuances of English to persuade, influence, and provoke thought. The examples of figures like Winston Churchill, Martin Luther King Jr., and Malala Yousafzai illustrate how language can transcend mere words to inspire action and change. Mastering the art of debating in English means not just speaking fluently but harnessing the power of expressions to wield influence over the hearts and minds of listeners.

CHAPTER FOUR

Elevating Your Speech: Effective Techniques Used by Commencement Speakers

Commencement speeches are a tricky business. They mark a milestone moment—be it the end of academic life or the beginning of a new chapter—yet they must be more than just formal platitudes. The best commencement speeches engage the audience, offering insights while remaining entertaining. Some are memorable for their wisdom, others for their wit, and many for their humor and relatability. The trick for any speaker lies in making the audience laugh, reflect, and leave inspired. This chapter will explore effective techniques used by some of the best commencement speakers, spiced up with funny stories and humorous examples that add life to their delivery.

1. The Power of Storytelling

A good story can turn a forgettable speech into an unforgettable experience. Storytelling is a common device in commencement speeches because it allows speakers to connect with the audience on a personal level. Through anecdotes, speakers can offer lessons in an engaging way. A commencement address without a story is like a stand-up comedy routine without jokes—doomed to fall flat.

Consider Steve Jobs' famous 2005 Stanford commencement speech. Jobs shared three personal stories about life, death, and connecting the dots. One particularly poignant story was about dropping out of college, only to "drop in" on a calligraphy class that seemed useless at the time but later became the foundation for Apple's beautiful typography. The lesson? Sometimes what seems like a pointless detour is a crucial part of your life's journey.

But it's not just about deep wisdom. Take comedian Ellen DeGeneres, who spoke at Tulane University in 2009. She began by sharing her story of growing up and dreaming of becoming a veterinarian before realizing how much she disliked school. She then delivered the punchline, "Then I decided I wanted to be an actress because that's a much more practical pursuit." The humor allowed the students to connect, laugh, and feel that even successful people have their share of odd career decisions.

Funny Example: Imagine you're sitting in the audience at a graduation ceremony. The speaker starts with a story: "When I was graduating, I had a simple plan: make a million dollars in a year, retire by 30, and travel the world. Fast forward to today—I'm still broke, live in my parents' basement, and my most exotic travel destination is Costco." Everyone laughs because it's relatable. The point isn't the failure of the plan, but the lesson learned along the way. Stories like these disarm the audience and provide humor with a deeper message.

2. Self-Deprecating Humor

Self-deprecating humor is a surefire way to win over an audience. By poking fun at their own mistakes or shortcomings, commencement speakers demonstrate humility and relatability. Instead of putting themselves on a pedestal, they stand beside the graduates, showing that no one has everything figured out.

One of the most famous examples of this technique is Conan O'Brien's Harvard commencement speech in 2000. In his classic style, Conan mocked his own career by recounting how his dream to host "The Tonight Show" led to what he called a "massive, public humiliation" after NBC replaced him with Jay Leno. He quipped, "Harvard, today, has been generous enough to bestow on me an honorary degree. You are Harvard! I am Conan—we both went to

Harvard, we are equals... except for the income thing." His ability to laugh at his misfortune made him relatable and endearing while subtly offering the lesson that setbacks are a part of life.

Funny Example: Imagine a speaker opening with, "When I was your age, I was much like you—full of hopes, dreams, and a can-do spirit. Unfortunately, I was also full of pizza and terrible ideas. One time, I thought I could 'follow my passion' and make a living by reviewing fast-food restaurants. Spoiler alert: You can't. My life has since been a long chain of poor decisions, but the good news is, I'm still here to tell the tale, so you can do better." This form of humor works wonders because it immediately humanizes the speaker and sets a relaxed tone for the speech.

3. Embracing Awkwardness and Relatability

Graduates sitting in their gowns may be thinking, "What happens next? How do I adult?" Commencement speeches often capitalize on this awkward life stage by acknowledging that the world beyond school is unpredictable and often uncomfortable. Addressing this awkwardness head-on makes the speaker more relatable.

Take Mindy Kaling's commencement address at Dartmouth College in 2018. She hilariously recounted how, after graduating, she thought she would finally have her life together. "But guess what? You're never going to 'have it all together.' It's all a scam!" Kaling admitted that even now, with all her success, she was still figuring things out. "The scary news is: you're on your own now. The good news is: No one has any idea what they're doing either." She used humor to relieve the anxiety many graduates feel, wrapping it in a reassuring message.

Funny Example: Imagine a speaker saying, "As graduates, you now hold the power to change the world! And by 'change the world,' I mean you'll spend the next six months filling out job applications while explaining to your parents that 'a gap year' is a perfectly valid life choice." The speaker uses humor to acknowledge the awkwardness of post-college life, helping students laugh off their fears of what comes next.

4. Playing with Language and Wordplay

Wordplay and linguistic humor are great tools in a commencement speaker's arsenal. Puns, metaphors, and humorous twists on common phrases can add levity to what might otherwise feel like a heavy, serious speech. A well-timed pun or clever word choice can engage an audience and make the speech more memorable.

For example, in his address to Kenyon College, David Foster Wallace famously opened with, "Two fish are swimming along, and one fish says to the other, 'How's the water?' The second fish replies, 'What the hell is water?'" It's an amusing and seemingly absurd story, but it became the anchor for his deep exploration of the importance of awareness and perspective in daily life.

Funny Example: A commencement speaker might say, "Graduation is a lot like taking off a Band-Aid. It feels good once it's over, but for now, it might sting a little—especially if your Band-Aid is made of student loans." This kind of play on words turns a serious issue into a light-hearted moment while still acknowledging the reality of life post-college.

5. Embracing the Absurd

One of the most unexpected and effective techniques in commencement speeches is embracing absurdity. Speakers who allow themselves to be goofy or playful with their audience create a sense of camaraderie. Humor rooted in the absurd acknowledges that not everything has to be serious to be meaningful.

Consider actor Will Ferrell's commencement speech at USC in 2017. Ferrell took the absurd to new levels, at one point breaking into song to serenade the graduates with Whitney Houston's "I Will Always Love You." His absurd humor was not just about getting laughs but making the moment memorable. "By the way, if you're thinking about getting into the movie business, don't! It's very hard!" Ferrell's willingness to embrace the ridiculous not only entertained but also lightened the mood, making his life advice more digestible.

Funny Example: Imagine a speaker addressing graduates with, "Now, let me share the ancient secret to success. Leans in close, whispers: It's just... winging it! Really, most of us are making it up as we go along. If anyone tells you otherwise, they're probably trying to sell you a course for $299.99 on 'How to Achieve Overnight Success.'" The absurdity of the statement is humorous, but it also conveys a deeper truth about life's unpredictability and the myth of a 'one-size-fits-all' approach to success.

6. Turning Conventional Wisdom on Its Head

Many commencement speeches rely on familiar tropes: Follow your passion. Work hard. Don't give up. But the best speakers know how to twist these clichés in new and humorous ways to surprise their audience and keep them engaged.

Take author Neil Gaiman's 2012 commencement speech at the University of the Arts, where he encouraged graduates not to be afraid of making mistakes. "If you're making mistakes, it means you're out there doing something," Gaiman said. He then added, "And some of you, I hope, will go out and make spectacular mistakes. Break rules. Leave the world more interesting for your being here." By flipping the traditional advice—avoid mistakes—on its head, Gaiman created a more refreshing and empowering message.

Funny Example: A speaker might say, "They tell you to 'follow your passion.' Well, let me tell you, my passion was binge-watching Netflix and eating Doritos, and it didn't get me very far. So maybe don't always follow your passion. Sometimes, follow your brain. It's there for a reason." This humorous twist on traditional advice leaves the audience laughing while giving them a more balanced perspective.

7. The Mix of Humor and Inspiration

Commencement speeches are unique opportunities for speakers to impart wisdom while celebrating an important moment in graduates' lives. The most effective speeches use humor, storytelling, and clever language to elevate their messages. From self-deprecating humor to absurdity, speakers like Conan O'Brien, Ellen DeGeneres, and Will Ferrell have shown that comedy can coexist with inspiration. Whether it's poking fun at themselves or offering stories of failure and triumph, commencement speakers succeed when they keep their audience engaged and entertained.

So, the next time you find yourself tasked with giving a speech—whether it's to a crowd of graduates or just a room full of your friends—remember: don't be afraid to make them laugh. After all, humor isn't just a way to entertain; it's a way to connect, inspire, and elevate your message to a whole new level.

CHAPTER FIVE

The Authority of News: Exploring Vocabulary Used by BBC News Readers

Ah, the BBC News. For many, it's the epitome of authority, calmness, and poise. The newsreaders on the BBC sit behind their shiny desks, reading the headlines with the grace of seasoned diplomats and the diction of a Shakespearean actor delivering Hamlet's soliloquy. But what exactly is it about the way these BBC newsreaders speak that makes us trust them so deeply? Is it the impeccable pronunciation? The formal tone? Or perhaps it's the vocabulary—those particular words that make everything, even the most chaotic news, sound so... dignified.

Let's take a fun, light-hearted look at the vocabulary used by BBC newsreaders, sprinkle in some humor, and uncover the secret sauce that makes them the Guardians of Seriousness in a world full of clickbait and chaos.

1. The Elegant Use of Understatement

If there's one thing BBC newsreaders excel at, it's the delicate art of understatement. You know, the ability to describe absolute mayhem in the most composed and restrained way possible. When the world is falling apart, the BBC is there to describe it with a soothing tone and a vocabulary that gently cushions the blow.

Consider this classic example: "The situation in Parliament today was somewhat tense." Translation: There were riots in the streets, MPs were throwing shoes at each other, and someone's toupee flew off during an impassioned debate.

Or, "The economic outlook for the country appears challenging." What they mean is, "Grab your pitchforks, there's no bread left, and the currency is now only good for origami lessons."

It's as if the BBC's rulebook says, "Thou shalt never describe anything as 'bad'—rather, opt for gentler terms like unfortunate, concerning, or problematic." You could almost imagine BBC newsreaders describing the sinking of the Titanic as, "There was an incident involving an iceberg. Passengers were mildly inconvenienced by an unexpected dip in the water."

Joke Example: Imagine the BBC newsreader saying, "There was some disruption on the London Underground today," which, in real terms, means, "The entire city of London descended into a post-apocalyptic wasteland of commuter chaos. There were no survivors."

2. The Curious Vocabulary of 'Crisis'

Speaking of understatement, nothing embodies this better than the BBC's approach to crises. But the word crisis is itself a curious thing in BBC-land. You'll almost never hear it said alone. No, no—that would be too straightforward. A crisis must always come with a disclaimer: potential crisis, emerging crisis, imminent crisis. This is the BBC's way of saying, "It's not a crisis yet, but keep your teacups at the ready, things might get slightly unpleasant soon."

The vocabulary of crisis is delicate. You don't want to scare people by saying things are disastrous, so you say, "There are growing concerns regarding the economic downturn." Translation: People are panicking and hiding their money in their mattresses.

Let's not forget the famous phrase in turmoil. It's never full-blown chaos. The world might be burning, but on the BBC, it's just "in turmoil." "The political landscape is in turmoil," they'll say, as if it's simply having a bad hair day.

Joke Example: BBC Newsreader: "The country is facing a potential crisis due to an incoming meteor." Translation: The meteor is the size of Texas, but for now, let's call it mildly concerning. At least until it actually hits. Then we'll upgrade it to a rather significant inconvenience."

3. Adjectives That Mean the Opposite of What You Think

If there's one thing BBC newsreaders love, it's using adjectives in ways that don't quite match up to reality. It's a delightful quirk of their vocabulary. Consider the word interesting. When a BBC newsreader describes something as "an interesting development," you might assume it's something worth paying attention to. In truth, it usually means, "This is the most boring thing that's ever happened, but we have to talk about it because it's our job."

And then there's remarkable. Now, when I hear "remarkable," I expect something jaw-dropping—like the discovery of a new planet or cats learning to use power tools. But when the BBC says, "This is a remarkable turn of events," it means someone in Parliament changed their tie, and we're all supposed to care.

Let's also talk about unprecedented. This word gets thrown around by BBC newsreaders more than cake at a birthday party. "This is an unprecedented situation," they'll say, even if the same thing happened last year, and the year before that, and—oh look, in 1985. Everything is unprecedented—or, at least, that's what they'd like us to believe.

Joke Example: BBC Newsreader: "In a truly unprecedented move, the government has decided to delay the vote once again." Translation: This happens every single time, but saying unprecedented makes it sound exciting, like the start of a heist movie.

4. The Politely Neutral Phraseology

One of the best things about BBC newsreaders is how they use polite, neutral language to navigate around politically sensitive topics. They never say, "This politician was caught lying." Instead, they'll say, "The minister's statements were inconsistent with the facts." Isn't that just a beautiful, non-accusatory way of calling someone out?

When it comes to scandals, too, the vocabulary is impeccably neutral. You won't hear the word scandal on BBC News. Instead, it's a controversy, or better yet, a situation. The word allegedly is their favourite shield, used liberally to deflect anything that might sound too definitive. You could have video evidence of a politician stealing the crown jewels, and the BBC would say, "The individual allegedly engaged in activities involving questionable behaviour."

This diplomatic language extends to international affairs. During wars, for example, you won't hear about "bombings" or "attacks"; it'll be "military operations" or "airstrikes"—much softer, almost as if they're discussing a neighbourhood football match.

Joke Example: BBC Newsreader: "The Prime Minister's involvement in the incident is under scrutiny." Translation: They caught him red-handed, but we'll call it scrutiny because under arrest sounds too harsh.

5. The Majestic Use of Passive Voice

Ah, the passive voice, a staple in BBC vocabulary. It's a linguistic masterpiece designed to tell you everything and nothing at the same time. If something goes wrong, BBC newsreaders won't say, "The government made a mistake." Instead, they'll say, "Mistakes were made." Notice how no one is to blame? It's magical. The mistake just... appeared! Out of nowhere! Mistakes were made, but no human had anything to do with it. It's like a mistake fairy came down and sprinkled errors all over the place.

You can also expect phrases like "It is believed that..." or "It has been suggested that..." Who believes it? Who suggested it? No one knows! But rest assured, someone, somewhere, said it, and the BBC is reporting it with their signature vagueness.

Joke Example: BBC Newsreader: "It has been reported that a significant error occurred during the negotiations." Translation: They messed up big time, but we're not going to name names. The error probably has its own Netflix series by now.

6. Using Very Formal Words for Mundane Events

BBC newsreaders have a delightful habit of using the most formal language possible to describe the most mundane events. While most of us would say, "It's raining," the BBC will inform you, "The region is experiencing precipitation." If there's a bit of wind, it's not just a windy day; the BBC will declare, "Winds are reaching gusting speeds of 20 miles per hour."

Even sports are given this elevated treatment. Where an ordinary sports commentator might say, "The player missed the shot," the BBC would say, "The player's attempt was unsuccessful." It's like they're trying to turn a missed free throw into a Shakespearean tragedy.

Joke Example: BBC Newsreader: "The match concluded with a scoreline that did not favour the home side." Translation: They lost. Badly. It was a disaster. But we're going to describe it as though it's an ancient Greek drama.

7. The Timeless Use of the Word 'Meanwhile'

If you've ever watched BBC News, you'll know that no news segment is complete without the word meanwhile. It's their go-to transition word for connecting unrelated stories. "Meanwhile, in other news..." This makes you feel like they've been patiently waiting to let you in on this juicy bit of information, even if it's something entirely unrelated—like jumping from a story about the stock market to a penguin in Antarctica finding a new friend.

"Meanwhile" is their way of saying, "We're done with that depressing story, here's something else, equally vague but with the same air of importance."

Joke Example: BBC Newsreader: "Meanwhile, a dog in Dorset has made headlines by learning to skateboard." Translation: We don't have any more serious news, but hey, look! A dog on wheels! Isn't that delightful?

The BBC's news vocabulary is like a comforting cup of tea in a storm. It's formal, understated, and loaded with a delightful combination of vagueness and authority. Through their clever use of words, BBC newsreaders manage to make even the most dramatic events sound like an invitation to afternoon tea. And, if you listen carefully, you'll catch the subtle humour in the language itself—the formal phrases and passive constructions that let you know they're taking things seriously, even when they probably shouldn't.

So, the next time you tune in to the BBC, pay attention to those interesting turns of phrase, those slightly problematic crises, and remember: no matter how bad things get, the BBC will always find a way to make it sound like a remarkable turn of events!

CHAPTER SIX

Commanding Attention: Techniques Employed by Orators and Public Speakers

Public speaking is an art that has shaped history, inspired movements, and left lasting impacts on audiences. Great orators are not merely individuals who speak; they are those who command attention, captivate listeners, and stir emotions. Whether delivering a rousing political speech, motivating a team, or giving a heartwarming toast, certain techniques consistently elevate speakers into the realm of the memorable. Let's dive into some of the most effective strategies used by master orators, and explore how they transform words into captivating performances.

1. The Power of the Pause

One of the most underrated yet powerful tools in public speaking is the pause. A well-timed pause can be more impactful than any word spoken. When a speaker pauses, they create anticipation, allowing the audience to digest what has been said, and encouraging them to lean in for what comes next. It breaks up the rhythm of speech and punctuates key moments, often amplifying the weight of the message.

Example: Take Martin Luther King Jr.'s famous "I Have a Dream" speech. Notice how he masterfully pauses after delivering powerful lines: "I have a dream... that one day..." The silence that follows each pause is like a spotlight, shining on his words and making them resonate deeply.

Pro Tip: Use pauses strategically to highlight important points. It's like giving your audience a moment to gasp, to let their minds catch up, and to anticipate your next gem of wisdom.

2. Storytelling: The Emotional Hook

Storytelling is the emotional core of great oratory. Humans are hardwired to love stories. They evoke emotion, transport us to different places, and make abstract ideas relatable. A powerful story can transform a mundane speech into a riveting experience. Whether it's a personal anecdote, a historical tale, or a metaphorical example, a well-told story gives the audience a narrative to latch onto.

Example: In Steve Jobs' 2005 Stanford commencement speech, he famously shared stories from his own life—his early struggles, dropping out of college, founding Apple, and getting fired from his own company. These stories weren't just entertaining; they were deeply relatable and filled with lessons. Jobs used these narratives to drive home points about perseverance, love, and following your passion.

Pro Tip: When preparing a speech, ask yourself: What story can I tell to illustrate my key points? Make it personal, vivid, and relevant to your audience's experience.

3. Rhetorical Questions: Engage the Audience's Mind

One effective way to keep an audience engaged is to ask rhetorical questions. These questions don't require a verbal response but prompt listeners to think, reflect, and become mentally involved in the speech. They break the passivity of just listening and invite the audience to think alongside the speaker.

Example: John F. Kennedy's inaugural address famously asked, "Ask not what your country can do for you—ask what you can do for your country." This rhetorical question immediately shifts focus from the government to the individual, challenging listeners to think about their role in public service.

Pro Tip: Sprinkle rhetorical questions throughout your speech to create moments of introspection. It keeps the audience on their toes and helps them connect their thoughts with your message.

4. Repetition: Driving the Message Home

Repetition is a time-tested rhetorical device that reinforces key points. When a phrase or idea is repeated, it becomes more memorable and impactful. Repetition creates a rhythm, building momentum that sweeps the audience along with it. But beware, it's a technique that can quickly become overused, so it must be employed sparingly and purposefully.

Example: Consider Winston Churchill's speech during World War II, where he famously repeated the phrase, "We shall fight," in various contexts. "We shall fight on the beaches, we shall fight on the landing grounds, we shall fight in the fields and in the streets..." Each repetition strengthens the resolve and determination, making the speech more stirring with each iteration.

Pro Tip: Use repetition when you want to emphasize a core theme or rally your audience around a particular idea. The more often you say it, the more it sticks.

5. Voice Modulation: Controlling Pitch and Tone

Great speakers know how to modulate their voice—they don't speak in a monotone. A good orator plays with the highs and lows, speed and intensity, allowing the voice to rise when delivering excitement or urgency and drop into softer tones when conveying serious, reflective moments. This keeps the speech dynamic and keeps the audience engaged.

Example: Barack Obama is a master of voice modulation. In his speeches, he seamlessly transitions from soft, contemplative tones to powerful crescendos, leaving the audience hanging on his every word. His pacing changes create emotional highs and lows that reflect the content of his speech.

Pro Tip: Practice your speech with varied tone and pitch. Imagine you're narrating a story to a child—use your voice to create atmosphere and drama. Lower your tone to express empathy or seriousness, and raise it to inspire or energize.

6. Body Language: Speak with Your Whole Self

Words are only part of communication. Body language plays a huge role in how a speaker's message is received. Confident speakers use gestures, facial expressions, and posture to complement their speech. They command attention not just with their words, but with how they physically present themselves. Stiff, unnatural movements can undermine your message, while fluid, purposeful gestures can emphasize key points.

Example: TED Talk speakers are renowned for their body language. Watch Amy Cuddy's TED Talk on body language, where her confident, open posture not only reinforces her ideas but becomes part of her message. Her gestures are aligned with her words, creating a cohesive and convincing argument.

Pro Tip: Use expansive gestures to convey openness and confidence. Make eye contact with different sections of your audience to create a personal connection, and avoid pacing too much—it can make you appear nervous.

7. Humor: The Universal Connector

Humor is one of the most effective tools in a speaker's arsenal. When done right, humor can break the ice, make the audience more comfortable, and help convey complex ideas in an accessible way. It shows the audience that you don't take yourself too seriously and establishes a more relaxed, human connection.

Example: At the White House Correspondents' Dinner, presidents often use humor to lighten the atmosphere. Barack Obama's 2015 speech included jabs at political opponents, self-deprecating humor, and even playful mockery of the media. This humor didn't detract from his authority; instead, it humanized him and connected him to the audience.

Pro Tip: Use humor that is appropriate for your audience and situation. Self-deprecating humor is often a safe bet—people appreciate when speakers don't take themselves too seriously. Just make sure your jokes don't distract from your message.

8. Call to Action: Mobilizing the Audience

A speech is often most powerful when it leaves the audience with a clear call to action. Great speakers don't just inform or entertain—they inspire action. Whether it's urging people to change their thinking, support a cause, or take a specific step, an effective call to action creates a sense of purpose.

Example: Greta Thunberg's impassioned speeches about climate change have a clear call to action: She urges world leaders and individuals alike to take immediate, drastic action to mitigate climate change. Her speeches are direct, urgent, and leave no room for complacency.

Pro Tip: End your speech with a call to action that is clear, direct, and actionable. Make it something the audience can realistically do, and inspire them to take that next step with passion and conviction.

9. Connecting with the Audience: Know Who You're Speaking To

Before you can command attention, you have to connect with your audience. Great speakers understand who their audience is, what they care about, and how to appeal to them. Whether it's through shared values, humor, or empathy, a connection must be established to make the audience feel like the speaker understands them.

Example: In his famous "Yes We Can" speech, Barack Obama used the phrase "we" to create a collective identity with his audience. He wasn't speaking to them; he was speaking with them, as though they were part of a shared mission.

Pro Tip: Tailor your speech to your audience's interests, values, and concerns. Use inclusive language like "we" and "us" to foster a sense of unity. Ask yourself: How can I make them feel like we're in this together?

10. Conclusion: The Power of the Grand Finale

The conclusion of a speech is where everything comes together. It's the last chance to leave an impression, so great orators always finish strong. Whether it's with a memorable quote, a final call to action, or a profound statement, the last words are often the most impactful.

Example: Abraham Lincoln's Gettysburg Address concluded with the powerful line, "...that government of the people, by the people, for the people, shall not perish from the earth." This timeless line, delivered at the end, remains one of the most iconic and remembered phrases in history.

Pro Tip: Your conclusion should echo the main theme of your speech and give the audience something to think about or act on. Don't let your energy or focus fade as you approach the end—finish with the same intensity and passion that you started with.

11. Bringing It All Together

Great orators combine these techniques to craft speeches that don't just inform but inspire, persuade, and resonate. By mastering the pause, using storytelling, asking rhetorical questions, playing with repetition, modulating your voice, engaging

CHAPTER SEVEN

Political Discourse: Mastering Vocabulary for Powerful Communication

Political discourse is more than just the exchange of ideas; it's about framing narratives, shaping opinions, and influencing audiences. In this context, vocabulary plays a pivotal role in conveying nuanced meaning and stirring emotions. Politicians, activists, and communicators in political spaces often use strategic language to galvanize support, debate policy, and shift public opinion. Mastering the vocabulary of political discourse is essential for anyone looking to communicate effectively in political spheres. This article delves into the key vocabulary and strategies to help you wield words with power and precision in political conversations.

1. Rhetoric: The Art of Persuasion

The term rhetoric refers to the art of using language effectively to persuade or influence. Politicians often use rhetoric to appeal to their audience's emotions, logic, or ethical values. Understanding rhetoric is vital for any political communicator.

Example: During the Civil Rights Movement, Martin Luther King Jr. employed rhetoric to appeal to American values of justice and equality in his famous "I Have a Dream" speech. His use of repetition and vivid imagery invoked both the logical argument for civil rights and the emotional desire for a united, equitable society.

Key Vocabulary:

- Ethos: Appeal to ethics or credibility.
- Pathos: Appeal to emotions.
- Logos: Appeal to logic or reason.

2. Framing: Shaping the Narrative

Framing refers to how issues are presented or structured to influence perception. By choosing certain words or perspectives, communicators can frame an issue in a way that benefits their position or challenges their opponents.

Example: Consider how debates around social welfare can be framed. Those in favor might use terms like "social safety net" to highlight compassion and support, while opponents might frame it as "government dependency" to focus on its potential drawbacks.

Key Vocabulary:

- Spin: The presentation of information in a biased way.
- Agenda: A hidden or overt plan guiding political action.
- Narrative: A coherent story or account shaping public perception.

3. Populism: Speaking for the People

Populist rhetoric aims to align with the common people, often by contrasting their interests with those of an elite or corrupt establishment. This is a powerful tool in political discourse, especially in times of discontent.

Example: A politician may appeal to populism by saying, "The elites in Washington have forgotten the hardworking people of this country." This positions them as a champion of the people against a distant or uncaring

ruling class.
Key Vocabulary:

- The Elite: A small, powerful group, often contrasted with the general population.
- The Establishment: The dominant political or economic class.
- Grassroots: Movements driven by the people, rather than by elites.

4. Dog Whistles: Covert Messaging

A dog whistle in politics refers to language that appears innocent on the surface but carries specific meaning for a targeted group. These phrases allow politicians to communicate to certain audiences without alienating others.

Example: A politician might say, "We need to protect traditional values," which could seem neutral but might signal to a conservative base a stance against social change, such as LGBTQ+ rights or immigration.

Key Vocabulary:

Coded language: Words or phrases that communicate a hidden message to a specific group.

Identity politics: Political positions based on the interests and perspectives of social groups with which people identify.

5. Euphemisms: Softening Harsh Realities

Euphemisms are words or phrases used to make something unpleasant sound more palatable. They are often employed in political discourse to downplay negative aspects of policies or situations.

Example: Instead of saying "civilian casualties," a government might refer to them as "collateral damage" during military conflicts. This softens the impact of the reality being described.

Key Vocabulary:

- Casualty: Victims, often in the context of war or conflict.
- Conflict: A less aggressive way to describe a war or military engagement.
- Enhanced interrogation: A euphemism for torture.

6. Demagoguery: Exploiting Prejudices

A demagogue is a leader who seeks support by appealing to popular desires, prejudices, or fears rather than by using rational argument. Demagogic language often inflames passions and sows division.

Example: During periods of economic instability, a demagogue might blame a particular group, such as immigrants, for society's problems, inciting anger and fear rather than focusing on the actual complexities of the situation.

Key Vocabulary:

- Inflammatory language: Words or phrases meant to provoke strong emotional reactions.
- Scapegoating: Blaming a particular person or group for problems.
- Xenophobia: Fear or hatred of foreigners or strangers.

7. Diplomacy: The Language of Negotiation

In contrast to inflammatory rhetoric, diplomatic language aims to soothe tensions and foster cooperation between parties. It often involves careful word choice to avoid offending others while advancing one's goals.

Example: During international negotiations, a diplomat might use phrases like, "We appreciate the concerns raised by our counterparts and will work towards a mutually beneficial solution," to keep discussions amicable and productive.

Key Vocabulary:

- Bilateral/multilateral talks: Negotiations between two or more parties or nations.

- Concessions: Compromises or adjustments made during negotiations.
- Sanctions: Punitive measures taken against a country to influence its actions.

8. Polarization: Dividing the Debate

Polarization refers to the growing division between opposing sides in a political debate. When discourse becomes polarized, compromise becomes more difficult, and both sides may use more extreme language to mobilize their base.

Example: In highly polarized environments, issues such as climate change may see one side labeling the other as "science deniers" while being branded as "alarmists" in return. This creates entrenched positions with little room for discussion.

Key Vocabulary:

- Partisan: Strong allegiance to one's political party, often leading to unwillingness to compromise.
- Echo chamber: Situations where people are only exposed to information or opinions that reinforce their own views.
- Tribalism: Loyalty to a political group or cause, often to the detriment of considering alternative viewpoints.

9. Oratory: Powerful Public Speaking

Oratory is the art of delivering speeches with eloquence and power. Great orators know how to craft their language to inspire, persuade, and mobilize large groups of people. In political discourse, the tone, pacing, and delivery of speeches are just as important as the words themselves.

Example: Winston Churchill's speeches during World War II, such as "We shall fight on the beaches," are iconic examples of political oratory. His use of defiant, resolute language inspired a nation under siege to keep fighting against overwhelming odds.

Key Vocabulary:

- Proclamation: A formal, public announcement.
- Declaration: A formal statement, often with political or legal weight.
- Call to action: A direct appeal to the audience to take action on an issue.

10. Appeals to Nationalism

Nationalism refers to a strong identification with one's nation, often to the exclusion of foreign influence. Politicians may use nationalistic rhetoric to rally support, especially during times of external threats or internal challenges.

Example: During Brexit debates, nationalist rhetoric was central, with slogans like "Take back control" and appeals to British sovereignty and independence from European Union regulations.

Key Vocabulary:

- Sovereignty: The authority of a state to govern itself.
- Patriotism: Pride in one's country.
- Isolationism: A policy of remaining apart from the affairs or interests of other groups, particularly in international relations.

11. Legitimacy and Authority

In political discourse, words related to legitimacy and authority determine who has the right to govern and how decisions should be made. Legitimacy refers to the general belief that a government or leader has the right to rule, while authority refers to the power or right to give orders.

Example: After elections, it's common to hear the phrase "a mandate from the people," which suggests that the winning party has earned the legitimacy to carry out its platform.

Key Vocabulary:

- Mandate: Authority granted by a constituency to act on its behalf.
- Constitutionality: Whether a law or action is in accordance with a constitution.
- Rule of law: The principle that all members of a society, including its leaders, are subject to the law.

Conclusion

Mastering the vocabulary of political discourse is essential for anyone who wants to engage in meaningful political communication. Whether you are a politician, activist, journalist, or concerned citizen, understanding how to use language effectively can help you navigate complex debates, influence public opinion, and advocate for your beliefs. The words you choose shape not only how you are perceived but also how your ideas resonate with others. By mastering rhetorical techniques, understanding how to frame issues, and knowing the emotional and logical appeals that work best in political contexts, you can become a more powerful and persuasive communicator.

CHAPTER EIGHT

Precision and Clarity: Strengthening Your Vocabulary for Effective Writing

In writing, the ability to convey thoughts with precision and clarity is essential. The words you choose shape how your readers understand and engage with your message. Often, writers fall into the trap of using vague, overcomplicated, or ambiguous language that clouds their communication. By strengthening your vocabulary with a focus on precision and clarity, you ensure that your writing is not only effective but also engaging.

This guide explores strategies to help you develop a more precise and clear vocabulary in your writing, along with examples and tips to enhance your communication.

1. Why Precision and Clarity Matter

Effective writing isn't just about what you say; it's about how you say it. Precision ensures that your readers understand your exact meaning, while clarity ensures that your message is straightforward and easy to follow. Miscommunication, ambiguity, and lack of coherence often stem from vague or imprecise language. On the other hand, precise and clear writing leaves no room for misinterpretation, making your ideas more persuasive and credible.

Example:

- **Vague:** The meeting was very long and important.
- **Precise:** The three-hour meeting addressed critical budget cuts for the upcoming fiscal year.

In the second sentence, the specifics of the meeting—its length and purpose—are clearly articulated, providing the reader with a complete understanding.

2. Avoiding Vague Words

Many words in the English language are vague and should be avoided if you're aiming for precision. Words like "thing," "very," "stuff," "something," or "nice" often obscure meaning rather than clarify it. Instead, strive to replace them with more specific words.

Example:

- **Vague:** She had a nice time at the conference.
- **Precise:** She enjoyed the keynote speech on sustainable energy practices at the conference.

The second sentence not only eliminates the vague word "nice" but also gives specific details about what made the experience enjoyable.

3. Be Concrete, Not Abstract

Concrete language refers to specific, tangible concepts, while abstract language deals with ideas that are harder to grasp. Abstract writing often leaves readers guessing, while concrete writing paints a clear picture.

Example:

- **Abstract:** The policy changes improved the company.

- **Concrete:** The new remote work policy increased productivity by 15% and reduced employee turnover by 10%.

By providing measurable outcomes and specific details, the second sentence gives a clearer understanding of how the company improved.

4. Choosing the Right Words (Synonyms and Shades of Meaning)

English is full of synonyms—words that have similar meanings but carry different connotations. Choosing the right synonym for the context is a key aspect of precision. While two words might technically mean the same thing, one might be more suitable than the other depending on the tone, audience, or context.

Example:

- **Irritate vs. Infuriate:** Both words describe anger, but "irritate" suggests mild annoyance, while "infuriate" implies intense anger.
- **Persuade vs. Convince:** While both words involve changing someone's mind, "persuade" usually involves influencing someone's actions, whereas "convince" focuses on changing their beliefs or thoughts.

Selecting the more appropriate word in each situation enhances both precision and tone.

5. Eliminating Redundancies

Redundancies occur when multiple words express the same idea, cluttering your writing. Identifying and eliminating redundancies is a simple yet effective way to improve clarity.

Examples:

- **Redundant:** The reason why he left is because he was unhappy.
- **Clear:** He left because he was unhappy.
- **Redundant:** In my personal opinion, I think the plan is effective.
- **Clear:** In my opinion, the plan is effective.

By removing unnecessary words, the writing becomes more concise and easier to follow.

6. Use Strong Verbs and Nouns

Weak verbs often rely on adverbs to convey meaning, while strong verbs and nouns stand on their own and pack more of a punch. By choosing stronger verbs and more specific nouns, you can eliminate the need for excessive modifiers, making your writing more precise.

Examples:

- **Weak:** She quickly ran across the street.
- **Strong:** She sprinted across the street.
- **Weak:** He gave a talk about climate change.
- **Strong:** He delivered a lecture on climate change.

In both examples, the strong verbs ("sprinted" and "delivered") replace weaker verbs that needed adverbs to add detail.

7. Watch for Ambiguity

Ambiguous sentences can confuse your readers and lead to misunderstandings. Ensuring that your sentences have one clear meaning will help avoid ambiguity.

Example:

- **Ambiguous:** He discussed the new policy with his manager and employees.
- **Clear:** He discussed the new policy with his manager and then explained it to the employees.

In the first sentence, it's unclear whether the manager and employees were part of the same conversation or if there were two separate discussions. The second sentence eliminates that ambiguity.

8. Use Transitions to Improve Coherence

Even when individual sentences are clear, your overall message can become muddled if your ideas don't flow well. Transition words and phrases help connect ideas, improving the clarity and coherence of your writing.

Examples:

- **Without transition:** The company implemented a new marketing strategy. Sales increased by 25%.
- **With transition:** After the company implemented a new marketing strategy, sales increased by 25%.

Transitions such as "after," "however," "moreover," and "consequently" help guide readers through your ideas and highlight relationships between them.

9. Cut Unnecessary Words

Brevity often leads to clarity. Many writers tend to use more words than necessary to convey their ideas. By trimming the fat from your sentences, you not only improve clarity but also make your writing more engaging.

Examples:

- **Wordy:** Due to the fact that the project was delayed, the team missed the deadline.
- **Concise:** Because the project was delayed, the team missed the deadline.
- **Wordy:** The new policy is in the process of being implemented by the team.
- **Concise:** The team is implementing the new policy.

Removing unnecessary words makes the writing more direct and impactful.

10. Use Analogies and Examples for Clarity

Sometimes, complex ideas need analogies, examples, or illustrations to be made clearer. While precise language is key, explaining difficult concepts with analogies or examples ensures that the reader grasps your message.

Example:

- **Without analogy:** The brain processes information through electrical signals transmitted by neurons.
- **With analogy:** The brain processes information like a computer, with neurons acting like wires that transmit electrical signals to different parts of the system.

The analogy helps break down a complex concept into something more familiar and easier to understand.

11. Be Specific

One of the most effective ways to strengthen your vocabulary for clarity is to be as specific as possible. Generalizations can make your writing sound vague and uncertain, while specific details make your writing stronger and more engaging.

Examples:

- **General:** Many people attended the event.
- **Specific:** Over 300 people attended the event.
- **General:** The book was interesting.
- **Specific:** The book provided fascinating insights into the psychological effects of social media on teenagers.

The second examples in both cases paint a much clearer picture for the reader.

12. Read and Revise

Effective writing is often a process of revision. Your first draft may not be as clear and precise as you'd like, but by revising, you can strengthen your vocabulary, eliminate ambiguity, and ensure clarity. Read your writing out loud or have someone else review it to catch areas where precision or clarity may be lacking.

Tip: After writing, set your work aside for a while before revising. Returning to it with fresh eyes can help you spot unnecessary words, vague language, or areas where clarity can be improved.

Conclusion

Strengthening your vocabulary for precision and clarity in writing is an ongoing process, but with the right strategies, you can dramatically improve how you communicate. Focus on eliminating vague words, choosing the right synonyms, using strong verbs, and ensuring specificity in your descriptions. By revising and cutting unnecessary words, you'll find that your writing becomes sharper, clearer, and more engaging for your readers. Whether you're writing an essay, a business report, or a creative piece, mastering precise and clear language will help you convey your message effectively and with confidence.

CHAPTER NINE

The Art of Storytelling: Weaving Powerful Expressions into Your Narratives

Storytelling is as ancient as humanity itself. From cave drawings to epic tales, stories have always been a means of connection, education, and entertainment. But what makes a story truly unforgettable? It's the art of expression. By mastering the use of vivid language, emotional depth, and a well-structured narrative, you can transform any tale into a mesmerizing experience. This chapter will guide you through the essential techniques to weave powerful expressions into your stories, enhancing your vocabulary and your ability to captivate an audience.

1. The Power of Descriptive Language

Descriptive language breathes life into your stories. It allows readers to see, hear, taste, touch, and feel the world you create. Consider the difference between "It was a sunny day" and "The golden rays of the sun poured over the horizon, warming the dewy grass." The latter paints a vivid picture that transports the reader to the scene.

Tips for Descriptive Writing

Expand Your Adjective Arsenal: Replace generic words like good, bad, or nice with more specific adjectives like phenomenal, atrocious, or charming.

Use Active Verbs: Instead of saying "She was walking slowly," opt for "She trudged through the cobblestone path."

Integrate Sensory Details: Describe how things look, sound, smell, taste, and feel.

2. Emotional Resonance Through Vocabulary

To connect with your audience on a deeper level, your narrative must evoke emotions. The choice of words can significantly impact the mood and tone of your story. Compare the phrases "He left the room quietly" and "He slipped away, his heart weighed down by unspoken words." The latter conveys a stronger emotional pull.

Building Emotional Vocabulary

Understand Emotional Nuance: Learn words that differentiate between similar emotions, such as melancholy versus despair.

Use Metaphors and Similes: "Her laughter was like a gentle breeze, carrying away the weight of the world."

Employ Repetition for Emphasis: Repetition of key phrases or ideas can amplify their emotional effect.

3. Structuring Your Narrative for Maximum Impact

Even the most vibrant expressions can fall flat without a well-organized story. A strong structure provides the framework that supports your creative language.

Elements of a Compelling Narrative

The Hook: Start with a sentence or idea that grabs attention immediately.

Conflict: Introduce a challenge or problem that drives the plot.

Climax: Build toward a peak moment of tension or revelation.

Resolution: Conclude with a satisfying end that ties up loose ends or leaves the audience in thoughtful contemplation.

4. Dialogues: Giving Voice to Your Characters

Realistic and engaging dialogues can bring characters to life. They reveal personalities, emotions, and relationships. Pay attention to the rhythm, tone, and choice of words in conversations.

Crafting Effective Dialogues

Reflect Character Personality: A scholarly character might say, "I find this development intriguing," while a casual one might say, "That's pretty cool."

Use Subtext: What's left unsaid can be as impactful as the spoken words.

Avoid Overloading with Information: Keep dialogues natural and to the point.

5. The Art of Pacing: Knowing When to Elaborate

Pacing determines how fast or slow a story unfolds. Too much detail can bog down a narrative, while too little can leave the reader confused or disinterested. Knowing when to use expansive vocabulary and when to simplify is key.

Balancing Pacing

Slow Down for Emotional Moments: Use vivid descriptions and introspection to delve into significant scenes.

Speed Up for Action: Use short, punchy sentences to heighten intensity.

6. Enriching Your Vocabulary for Storytelling

To truly master the art of storytelling, an extensive vocabulary is essential. However, vocabulary isn't just about knowing words—it's about using them effectively.

Ways to Expand Your Storytelling Vocabulary

Read Widely: Explore genres ranging from fantasy to biographies.

Maintain a Word Journal: Write down intriguing words and their meanings.

Experiment in Writing: Incorporate new words into short stories or journal entries.

7. Practicing the Craft

Storytelling, like any art, improves with practice. Experiment with different styles, genres, and perspectives. Revisit your narratives to refine the expressions and ensure they flow seamlessly.

Creative Exercises

Rewrite a Simple Story: Take a basic tale, like a fable, and rewrite it with rich descriptions and emotional depth.

Character Voice Exercise: Write a diary entry from the perspective of a character with a distinct personality.

Word Substitution: Take a paragraph and replace common words with more expressive synonyms.

The art of storytelling lies in the balance between creativity and technique. By weaving powerful expressions into your narratives, you not only enhance your storytelling abilities but also enrich your vocabulary. Remember, every word you choose has the power to transport, inspire, and move your audience. As you master this art, your stories will not just be read—they will be felt and remembered.

CHAPTER TEN

Adding Impact: Expressions That Create Strong Emotional Responses

Words and expressions hold immense power. They can evoke laughter, stir tears, or ignite fury. Mastering emotionally impactful language is essential for anyone looking to enhance their vocabulary and communicate with influence. This chapter delves into how carefully chosen expressions can amplify your message, resonate with your audience, and create unforgettable impressions.

The Science Behind Emotional Words

Language that triggers emotions taps into the limbic system, the brain's emotional hub. Words associated with strong feelings often bypass rational thought and connect directly with the listener's or reader's emotions. This is why emotional expressions are used in speeches, storytelling, marketing, and everyday conversations to leave a lasting impression.

Categories of Emotionally Impactful Expressions

To create strong emotional responses, it's important to understand the types of emotions words can evoke. Here are a few categories with examples:

1. Words of Joy and Celebration

Expressions of happiness and positivity often uplift and energize. For example:

Exuberant: "The crowd erupted in exuberant applause."

Euphoria: "Winning the championship was a moment of pure euphoria."

Radiant: "She looked radiant as she walked down the aisle."

2. Words of Fear and Alarm

Evoking fear or urgency can grab attention and provoke action:

Terrifying: "The sound of footsteps in the dark was utterly terrifying."

Catastrophic: "Ignoring the warning signs led to catastrophic consequences."

Imminent: "The danger was imminent, and there was no time to waste."

3. Words of Love and Compassion

Expressions of care and affection foster connection and warmth:

Endearing: "Her quirky habits made her even more endearing."

Tender: "He spoke in a tender voice, full of understanding."

Cherished: "The photograph was a cherished memory from her childhood."

4. Words of Anger and Resentment

Anger, when expressed skillfully, can emphasize the gravity of an issue:

Infuriating: "His blatant disregard for rules was infuriating."

Outrageous: "The outrageous behavior shocked everyone."

Scorn: "She could not hide the scorn in her voice."

5. Words of Sadness and Loss

Expressions of sorrow create depth and empathy:

Heartbreaking: "The story of the lost child was truly heartbreaking."

Melancholy: "There was a sense of melancholy in his goodbye."

Desolate: "She felt desolate in the empty house."

Techniques to Enhance Emotional Impact

1. Use Vivid Imagery:

Pair emotionally impactful words with imagery to make them more evocative. Instead of saying, "He was sad," say, "His face was etched with sorrow, and his eyes glistened with unshed tears."

2. Employ Metaphors and Similes:

Comparisons often deepen emotional resonance. For example:

Metaphor: "Her anger was a storm, unrelenting and destructive."

Simile: "He clung to hope like a drowning man to a lifeline."

3. Vary Sentence Structure:

Short sentences pack a punch, while longer ones build tension.

"She was gone. Forever." vs. "As the days turned into months, the reality of her absence began to sink in, leaving an ache that never faded."

4. Repetition for Emphasis:

Reiterating key phrases underscores emotion.

"He screamed. He screamed until his voice broke. He screamed until there was nothing left but silence."

5. Appeal to the Senses:

Incorporate sensory details to immerse your audience in the emotion.

"The aroma of freshly baked cookies flooded the room, a warm reminder of her grandmother's love."

Common Pitfalls to Avoid

Overloading Emotion:

Using too many emotional words can feel forced or melodramatic. Aim for balance.

Clichés:

Phrases like "a heavy heart" or "tears streaming down her face" can feel overused. Strive for originality.

Ignoring Context:

Emotionally charged words must fit the tone and context of the message. Overly dramatic expressions in a formal report, for instance, can be jarring.

Exercises to Build Your Emotional Vocabulary

1. Rewrite the Scene:

Take a neutral sentence like "He entered the room," and rewrite it to evoke specific emotions such as fear, joy, or sadness.

2. Word Pairing:

List emotions (e.g., happiness, anger) and find three impactful words for each.

3. Read and Analyze:

Read speeches, poems, or novels known for their emotional impact. Identify the words and techniques used.

Conclusion

The ability to use expressions that create strong emotional responses is a key skill for effective communication. By expanding your emotional vocabulary and applying it thoughtfully, you can captivate your audience, make your messages more memorable, and influence others profoundly. Remember, it's not just about what you say—it's about how you make others feel.

CHAPTER ELEVEN

Empathy and Connection: Vocabulary for Building Rapport and Understanding

Empathy is often described as the ability to understand and share the feelings of another, forming the foundation for meaningful human connection. In a world increasingly shaped by rapid technological advancements and social complexity, fostering empathy has become a cornerstone for personal and professional relationships. Words play a pivotal role in this process, acting as bridges that connect hearts and minds.

The Language of Empathy

Empathy begins with the ability to listen actively and respond with words that convey genuine care and understanding. Vocabulary that builds empathy includes terms that validate emotions, such as "I understand," "That sounds challenging," or "I can see why you feel that way." These phrases not only affirm the speaker's feelings but also create a safe space for deeper conversation.

For instance, Brené Brown, a renowned researcher on vulnerability and empathy, states, "Empathy is not connecting to an experience; it's connecting to the emotions that underpin an experience" (Brown 81). The emphasis on emotions underscores the importance of choosing words that resonate with another's emotional state, fostering a connection rooted in sincerity and respect.

Emotional Intelligence and Vocabulary

Empathy is a critical component of emotional intelligence, which involves recognizing, understanding, and managing emotions effectively. Words that reflect emotional intelligence often include those that acknowledge nuances, such as "confused," "overwhelmed," "hopeful," or "disheartened." By identifying specific emotions, individuals demonstrate their attentiveness and willingness to engage on a deeper level.

Daniel Goleman, a leading expert on emotional intelligence, asserts, "Effective communication is 20% what you know and 80% how you feel about what you know" (Goleman 42). This underscores that vocabulary used in empathetic communication must transcend surface-level interactions and delve into the emotional currents of a conversation.

Building Rapport Through Words

Rapport-the harmonious relationship marked by mutual understanding and trust—is essential for empathy. To build rapport, one must adopt language that mirrors the other person's sentiments. For example, phrases like "That's a great point," "Tell me more about that," or "I appreciate your perspective" demonstrate active interest and validation.

Furthermore, storytelling is a powerful tool for creating connections. Sharing personal anecdotes that relate to the other person's experience fosters a sense of camaraderie. As novelist Chimamanda Ngozi Adichie notes, "Stories have been used to dispossess and to malign. But stories can also be used to empower and to humanize" (Adichie 17). The right words, woven into relatable narratives, can break down barriers and build bridges of understanding.

The Role of Nonverbal Cues

While verbal vocabulary is crucial, nonverbal cues complement and reinforce empathetic communication. A warm tone of voice, open body language, and attentive eye contact amplify the impact of empathetic words. For example, saying "I'm here for you" with genuine warmth conveys deeper support than the words alone.

Albert Mehrabian's research highlights that "93% of communication is nonverbal" (Mehrabian 82). This finding emphasizes that empathy and connection require an integration of verbal and nonverbal expressions to fully resonate with others.

Cultural Sensitivity and Inclusivity

In our diverse world, empathy extends to embracing cultural differences and employing inclusive language. Words that respect cultural identities-such as using preferred pronouns or learning basic phrases in another's native language-convey respect and effort.

The late Maya Angelou encapsulates this idea, stating, "We all should know that diversity makes for a rich tapestry, and we must understand that all the threads of the tapestry are equal in value" (Angelou 54). By choosing vocabulary that acknowledges and celebrates diversity, individuals can foster a more inclusive and empathetic environment.

Avoiding Harmful Language

Equally important is the awareness of words that can harm or alienate. Avoiding phrases that dismiss or trivialize emotions, such as "It's not a big deal" or "You're overreacting," is essential. Empathetic communication requires sensitivity to the impact of words, ensuring they uplift rather than diminish.

Practicing Empathy Daily

Building a vocabulary for empathy is an ongoing process that involves practice and mindfulness. Techniques such as reflective listening, where one paraphrases what the speaker has shared, reinforce understanding. For example, responding with "What I hear you saying is..." not only clarifies meaning but also shows attentiveness.

Furthermore, reading literature and engaging with diverse perspectives can expand one's empathetic capacity. As Harper Lee writes in To Kill a Mockingbird, "You never really understand a person until you consider things from his point of view...until you climb into his skin and walk around in it" (Lee 39). Literature offers a lens through which we can explore the world's myriad experiences, enriching our empathetic vocabulary.

Conclusion

Empathy and connection hinge on the careful selection and delivery of words that foster understanding and rapport. By cultivating a vocabulary rich in emotional intelligence, inclusivity, and authenticity, individuals can navigate the complexities of human relationships with greater ease and compassion. As we refine our words and actions, we inch closer to building a world rooted in empathy, where every voice is heard, and every story matters.

Works Cited

Adichie, Chimamanda Ngozi. The Danger of a Single Story. TED, 2009.

Angelou, Maya. Wouldn't Take Nothing for My Journey Now. Random House, 1993.

Brown, Brené. Daring Greatly: How the Courage to Be Vulnerable Transforms the Way We Live, Love, Parent, and Lead. Gotham Books, 2012.

Goleman, Daniel. Emotional Intelligence: Why It Can Matter More Than IQ. Bantam Books, 1995.

Lee, Harper. To Kill a Mockingbird. J.B. Lippincott & Co., 1960.

Mehrabian, Albert. Silent Messages: Implicit Communication of Emotions and Attitudes. Wadsworth Publishing, 1971.

CHAPTER TWELVE

The Subtle Art of Diplomacy: Nuanced Vocabulary for Navigating Tricky Situations

In the labyrinth of interpersonal and professional interactions, diplomacy often acts as a guiding compass, helping individuals navigate complex dynamics with grace and tact. Mastering the subtle art of diplomacy is not merely about the words we choose, but the tone, context, and intention behind them. This chapter explores how nuanced vocabulary can de-escalate tension, build bridges, and foster understanding in challenging scenarios.

The Power of Words: Why Nuance Matters

Diplomatic language is akin to the brushstrokes of an artist; each word carries weight, subtly shaping perception and emotion. As Henry Wadsworth Longfellow aptly put it, "A torn jacket is soon mended; but hard words bruise the heart of a child" (Longfellow 67). In diplomacy, words are tools to heal and harmonize rather than hurt.

Consider the difference between saying, "You're wrong" and "Perhaps there's another perspective we can explore." While the former can alienate or provoke, the latter invites dialogue and mutual respect. Such phrasing not only preserves relationships but also facilitates problem-solving.

Key Phrases for Diplomacy

Acknowledging Diverse Perspectives:

"I understand your point, and I think it's worth exploring further."

"While I see where you're coming from, might I suggest another angle?"

De-escalating Conflicts:

"Let's take a step back and revisit this with fresh eyes."

"It seems there might have been a misunderstanding; let's clarify."

Proposing Solutions:

"How about we find a middle ground that works for everyone?"

"Would you be open to considering an alternative approach?"

The Role of Tone and Delivery

Nuanced vocabulary relies heavily on tone. A calm, measured voice can make even the most critical feedback feel constructive. As George Bernard Shaw observed, "The single biggest problem in communication is the illusion that it has taken place" (Shaw 89). Diplomacy ensures communication is not just spoken but also heard and understood.

Non-verbal cues, such as maintaining eye contact and open body language, reinforce the intent behind diplomatic words. A simple "Let's work on this together" accompanied by a reassuring smile can transform potential discord into collaboration.

Case Studies: Diplomatic Vocabulary in Action

Scenario 1: Workplace Disagreement

Imagine a team meeting where two colleagues are at odds over project priorities. Instead of taking sides or criticizing, a diplomatic leader might say:

"I see that both of you are deeply invested in the project's success, which is wonderful. Perhaps we can outline each priority's pros and cons and decide together on the best course of action."

This approach validates both viewpoints while steering the conversation toward a solution.

Scenario 2: Cultural Misunderstandings

During a cross-cultural negotiation, misinterpretations can occur. Phrases like "That's an interesting perspective" or "Can you help me understand this better?" demonstrate curiosity and respect, reducing the likelihood of offense.

The Ethics of Diplomacy

Diplomacy should never be confused with manipulation. While both involve strategic communication, manipulation seeks to deceive for personal gain, whereas diplomacy aims for mutual benefit. As Immanuel Kant stated, "Act only according to that maxim whereby you can, at the same time, will that it should become a universal law" (Kant 30). Ethical diplomacy ensures honesty and integrity are preserved while fostering goodwill.

Conclusion: Cultivating a Diplomatic Mindset

To master the art of diplomacy, one must develop empathy, patience, and a willingness to listen. Nuanced vocabulary serves as a bridge between intention and impact, transforming potential conflicts into opportunities for growth. As the adage goes, "Words are free. It's how you use them that may cost you." By choosing words with care and purpose, we can navigate the trickiest of situations with confidence and poise.

Works Cited

Kant, Immanuel. Groundwork of the Metaphysics of Morals. Translated by Mary Gregor, Cambridge University Press, 1998.

Longfellow, Henry Wadsworth. "The Children's Hour." The Complete Poetical Works of Henry Wadsworth Longfellow, Houghton Mifflin, 1893.

Shaw, George Bernard. Pygmalion and Three Other Plays. Penguin Classics, 2000.

CHAPTER THIRTEEN

Taking a Stand: Expressions for Asserting Your Opinion Confidently

In a world teeming with diverse perspectives and complex challenges, the ability to assert one's opinion confidently is not merely a skill but a necessity. Whether in professional environments, academic discussions, or social contexts, articulating thoughts clearly and convincingly can lead to meaningful dialogue, informed decisions, and societal progress. This chapter, "Taking a Stand: Expressions for Asserting Your Opinion Confidently," explores the art of confidently voicing opinions, the strategies for effective communication, and the tools needed to engage in respectful yet assertive discourse.

The Importance of Taking a Stand

Taking a stand involves expressing beliefs or opinions firmly and confidently. This ability is crucial for several reasons:

Promoting Self-Efficacy: Voicing one's thoughts reinforces self-belief and encourages personal growth.

Fostering Innovation: Sharing unique perspectives can spark new ideas and solutions.

Building Trust: Confidence in communication establishes credibility and fosters trust among peers.

Driving Change: History shows that assertive individuals often catalyze social, political, and organizational transformation.

However, taking a stand does not equate to being aggressive or dismissive. It requires a balance of confidence, empathy, and respect for differing viewpoints.

Foundations of Confident Expression

To assert an opinion confidently, one must develop foundational skills:

Self-Awareness: Understanding your values, beliefs, and biases is the first step toward articulating opinions authentically.

Critical Thinking: Analyze information critically to form well-rounded opinions backed by logic and evidence.

Effective Communication Skills: Mastering verbal and non-verbal communication is essential for delivering messages persuasively.

Emotional Intelligence: Recognizing and managing emotions in oneself and others helps navigate challenging discussions with empathy.

Expressions for Asserting Opinions

Confidently asserting opinions involves using language that conveys clarity, conviction, and respect. Below are categorized expressions to aid in different scenarios:

1. Starting Statements

Opening a discussion assertively sets the tone for confident expression. Examples include:

"In my opinion, it is essential to..."

"I firmly believe that..."

"From my perspective, the most logical approach is..."

"Based on the evidence, I would argue that..."

2. Supporting Arguments

Providing rationale strengthens your position. Examples:

"The primary reason for my stance is..."

"This is supported by data that shows..."

"To elaborate, the following factors are critical..."

"Historically, we have seen similar outcomes when..."

3. Addressing Counterarguments

Acknowledging opposing views while reinforcing your position demonstrates maturity and respect:

"While I understand the opposing viewpoint, I would argue that..."

"Some might suggest otherwise; however, the evidence indicates..."

"Although there is merit in that perspective, my concern is..."

"It is worth noting that despite these points, the broader implications suggest..."

4. Asserting Without Dismissiveness

Maintaining a respectful tone ensures constructive dialogue:

"I see your point; however, I would suggest considering..."

"That is an interesting perspective, and I'd like to add..."

"I respect your opinion but must point out..."

"While this approach has merits, I believe a more effective solution would be..."

5. Concluding Remarks

Ending a discussion assertively leaves a lasting impression:

"To conclude, my position is based on..."

"In summary, I strongly advocate for..."

"Ultimately, I believe the best course of action is..."

"To wrap up, my argument rests on the following principles..."

Strategies for Assertive Communication

Achieving confident expression requires more than memorizing phrases. It involves strategic application of communication principles:

1. Clarity and Conciseness

Avoid ambiguity. Articulate your points succinctly to ensure your audience grasps your position.

2. Use of Evidence

Substantiate your arguments with facts, data, or credible examples. This enhances your credibility and persuades others.

3. Adapting to the Audience

Tailor your language and approach based on the audience's knowledge level, preferences, and cultural context.

4. Non-Verbal Communication

Body language, tone of voice, and facial expressions significantly impact how your message is received. For instance:

Maintain eye contact to convey confidence.

Use an open posture to appear approachable.

Modulate your tone to reflect conviction without aggression.

5. Active Listening

Confident communication involves listening as much as speaking. Understanding others' viewpoints helps you address concerns and refine your arguments.

Overcoming Challenges in Asserting Opinions

Despite the benefits, asserting opinions confidently can be daunting. Common challenges include:

1. Fear of Judgment

- The fear of criticism often silences individuals. Overcoming this requires:
- Recognizing that differing opinions are natural.
- Focusing on the value of your contribution rather than potential reactions.

2. Lack of Preparation

- Unpreparedness undermines confidence. To mitigate this:
- Research thoroughly before expressing your opinion.
- Anticipate counterarguments and prepare responses.

3. Cultural and Social Barriers

- Cultural norms and societal expectations can hinder assertiveness. Navigating this involves:
- Respecting cultural sensitivities while staying true to your beliefs.
- Finding common ground to bridge differences.

4. Handling Aggression

- Confronting aggressive or dismissive behavior can be intimidating. Strategies include:
- Staying calm and composed.
- Redirecting the conversation to focus on facts and logic.
- Setting boundaries to maintain a respectful dialogue.
- Real-World Applications of Assertive Expression
- Confidently asserting opinions is invaluable in various contexts:

1. Professional Settings

- Presenting ideas in meetings.
- Negotiating with stakeholders.
- Advocating for policy changes or organizational improvements.

2. Academic Environments

- Participating in debates and discussions.
- Defending theses or research findings.
- Challenging existing theories or viewpoints constructively.

3. Social Interactions

- Addressing societal issues or injustices.
- Facilitating community discussions.
- Voicing concerns in group settings.

4. Personal Relationships

- Setting boundaries respectfully.
- Resolving conflicts with clarity and empathy.
- Expressing needs and preferences without hesitation.
- Inspiring Examples of Assertive Expression

Throughout history, individuals who confidently voiced their opinions have shaped societies. Examples include:

- Mahatma Gandhi: Advocated for non-violent resistance with unwavering conviction.
- Malala Yousafzai: Asserted the right to education despite life-threatening opposition.
- Martin Luther King Jr.: Delivered impassioned speeches that championed civil rights and equality.
- Greta Thunberg: Boldly called for climate action, inspiring global movements.

These figures demonstrate that confident expression can influence change, inspire action, and leave a lasting impact.

Tools and Resources for Building Confidence

Building confidence in asserting opinions requires practice and the right resources:

1. Public Speaking Workshops

Participate in workshops or clubs like Toastmasters to hone your communication skills.

2. Mindfulness and Stress Management

Practice techniques like meditation and deep breathing to manage anxiety and stay composed.

3. Feedback Mechanisms

Seek constructive feedback from peers, mentors, or coaches to improve your delivery.

4. Learning Platforms

Leverage online courses, books, and articles on communication, critical thinking, and debate skills.

To conclude, taking a stand and confidently asserting your opinion is a transformative skill that empowers individuals to influence decisions, foster dialogue, and drive progress. By mastering expressions for confident communication, embracing strategic approaches, and overcoming challenges, anyone can assert their opinions with clarity, conviction, and respect. In doing so, they contribute to a more informed, inclusive, and innovative world. Let this chapter serve as a guide and inspiration to take a stand, voice your truth, and make your mark.

CHAPTER FOURTEEN

Inspiring Others: Vocabulary That Motivates and Ignites Passion

Words hold immense power. They have the ability to uplift, inspire, and drive people toward greatness. The vocabulary we choose can be a spark that lights a fire in others, motivating them to achieve the extraordinary. This chapter explores the art of inspiring others through language, focusing on words and expressions that ignite passion, foster belief, and cultivate resilience. Whether you're leading a team, mentoring an individual, or addressing a crowd, the ability to inspire through words is a skill that can transform lives.

The Psychology of Inspiration

To inspire others effectively, it's essential to understand the psychological underpinnings of motivation and passion. Humans are wired to respond to narratives, emotions, and a sense of purpose. When we feel connected to a cause, we find the strength to overcome obstacles and achieve remarkable feats.

- Appealing to Values: Words that resonate with an individual's core beliefs and values create a deeper emotional connection.
- Triggering Emotion: Inspirational language often invokes emotions such as hope, pride, or determination.
- Creating Vision: People are inspired when they can visualize a future where their efforts lead to meaningful change.

Key Elements of Inspirational Vocabulary

1. Empowerment

Empowering words instill confidence and a sense of capability. Examples include:

- "You have the power to change the world."
- "Believe in your ability to overcome any challenge."

2. Action-Oriented Language

Dynamic verbs inspire movement and action. Examples include:

- "Take the first step toward your dreams."
- "Unleash your potential and seize this moment."

3. Visionary Phrases

Visionary expressions create a picture of an extraordinary future. Examples include:

- "Imagine a world where everyone thrives."
- "Together, we can shape a brighter tomorrow."

Inspiring in Different Contexts

1. In Leadership

Leaders inspire through clarity of purpose and a compelling vision. The use of inclusive language such as "we," "together," and "our" fosters unity and collective strength.

Example:

"As a team, we will break barriers and achieve what once seemed impossible."

2. In Education

Educators have the unique opportunity to inspire curiosity and lifelong learning. Encouraging students with affirmations like "Your ideas matter" or "You have the potential to innovate" fosters confidence and growth.

3. In Personal Mentorship

One-on-one interactions allow for tailored motivational language. Understanding an individual's aspirations and struggles makes your words more impactful.

Example:

"I see great potential in you. Your dedication and resilience will take you far."

The Power of Storytelling

Stories have a unique ability to inspire. They captivate attention, evoke emotions, and convey complex ideas in an accessible way. Inspirational storytellers often use:

- Personal Triumphs: Sharing how challenges were overcome can motivate others to persevere.
- Universal Themes: Stories of courage, love, and determination resonate universally.
- Vivid Imagery: Descriptive language brings stories to life, making them unforgettable.

Example:

"There was a time when I doubted myself, but through persistence and faith, I discovered that failure is not the end—it's a stepping stone to success."

Vocabulary of Inspiration

Here are categories of words and phrases that inspire action, ignite passion, and foster belief:

1. Words of Belief:

"Capable," "Resilient," "Fearless," "Determined," "Innovative."

2. Phrases of Motivation:

"Push beyond your limits."

"Rise above the ordinary."

"You are destined for greatness."

3. Expressions of Unity:

"Together, we can achieve the extraordinary."

"United by purpose, driven by passion."

4. Affirmations of Possibility:

"Anything is possible."

"Your dreams are within reach."

Techniques for Inspiring Communication

1. Use of Repetition

Reiterating key messages reinforces their importance and impact.

Example:

"We are strong. We are capable. We are unstoppable."

2. Powerful Openings and Closings

Begin with a statement that grabs attention and end with a call to action that lingers in the mind.

Opening Example:

"What if I told you that one idea could change the world?"

Closing Example:

"Go forth and make your mark on history."

3. Metaphors and Analogies

Comparisons create relatability and deeper understanding.

Example:

"Life is a canvas, and you hold the brush—paint it with bold strokes."

Practical Exercises for Building Inspirational Vocabulary

1. Daily Affirmation Practice

Write and repeat affirmations daily to internalize positive language.

Example:

"I am capable of inspiring others through my words."

2. Story Compilation

Create a collection of inspiring stories from history, personal experiences, or literature to draw upon when needed.

3. Role-Playing Scenarios

Practice delivering motivational speeches in varied contexts, such as leadership, mentorship, or education.

Thus, inspiring others through words is both an art and a science. By understanding the psychology of motivation, mastering key elements of inspirational vocabulary, and practicing effective communication techniques, you can ignite passion and drive meaningful change. Remember, the words you choose today can shape the dreams and actions of tomorrow. Speak with purpose, and inspire with conviction.

CHAPTER FIFTEEN

Words that Persuade: Manipulating Language to Influence Others

Language is a powerful tool, not merely a medium of communication but a mechanism through which minds can be shaped and decisions influenced. Persuasion is both an art and a science, where carefully chosen words can turn hesitation into action, doubt into certainty, and resistance into agreement. This chapter delves into the intricacies of persuasive language, exploring how it can be wielded effectively to influence others, build consensus, and drive meaningful outcomes.

Understanding Persuasion

Persuasion is the process of guiding someone to adopt a belief, attitude, or course of action. It is deeply rooted in psychology, leveraging emotional appeal, logical reasoning, and credibility to achieve its objectives.

Key Psychological Principles of Persuasion:

- Reciprocity: People tend to return favors, making words of gratitude and generosity powerful tools.
- Scarcity: Highlighting limited availability can create urgency and desirability.
- Authority: Referencing expertise or credibility instills trust and increases compliance.
- Consistency: Encouraging alignment with prior commitments fosters agreement.
- Social Proof: Demonstrating widespread acceptance or endorsement influences decisions.

Elements of Persuasive Language

1. Clarity and Precision

Persuasion begins with clarity. Ambiguity weakens arguments, while precise language ensures that the message resonates and is easily understood. For example:

Unclear: *"This might be a good idea."*

Clear: *"This strategy will significantly enhance our results."*

2. Emotive Words

Emotional appeal often outweighs logic in persuasive efforts. Words that evoke feelings of hope, fear, pride, or belonging are particularly impactful. Examples include:

"Imagine the joy of achieving this goal."

"Don't let this rare opportunity slip away."

3. Powerful Verbs

Action-oriented verbs drive momentum and encourage engagement. Examples include:

"Transform your career with this program."

"Empower yourself to make a difference."

4. Inclusive Language

Using pronouns like "we," "us," and "our" fosters a sense of unity and shared purpose.

"Together, we can achieve extraordinary results."

5. Rhetorical Questions

Posing questions engages the audience and leads them to draw desired conclusions. For example:

"Who wouldn't want to succeed with less effort?"

Techniques for Persuasion

1. The Rule of Three

Grouping information in sets of three enhances memorability and impact.

"This product is reliable, affordable, and effective."

2. Contrasting

Presenting a lesser alternative alongside the desired choice makes the latter more appealing.

"You can settle for average results, or you can embrace excellence."

3. Storytelling

Stories create emotional connections and make abstract ideas relatable.

Example:

"When Sarah implemented this approach, she doubled her sales in just three months."

4. Repetition

Repeating key messages reinforces them and ensures retention.

"Act now to secure your future. Act now to achieve your dreams."

Persuasion in Different Contexts

1. In Marketing

Marketing thrives on persuasive language that convinces consumers of a product's value. Techniques such as testimonials, limited-time offers, and aspirational messaging are commonly employed.

Example:

"Join the thousands who have transformed their lives with our program."

2. In Negotiations

Negotiators use persuasive language to find common ground and achieve mutually beneficial outcomes.

Example:

"By agreeing to this proposal, you gain unparalleled access to new markets."

3. In Leadership

Leaders inspire action and commitment through visionary and motivational language.

Example:

"Let's embark on this journey together, where every effort brings us closer to greatness."

Words and Phrases That Persuade

1. Words of Urgency:

"Now," "Limited," "Exclusive," "Immediate."

2. Words of Assurance:

"Guaranteed," "Proven," "Reliable," "Safe."

3. Words of Aspiration:

"Achieve," "Elevate," "Transform," "Inspire."

4. Phrases of Influence:

"Don't miss out on this opportunity."

"Imagine the possibilities."

"Take the first step today."

Ethical Considerations

While the power of persuasive language is undeniable, it must be used responsibly. Manipulating language to deceive or exploit others is unethical and can lead to loss of trust and credibility.

Guidelines for Ethical Persuasion:

- Be truthful and transparent.
- Respect the autonomy of your audience.
- Aim for mutually beneficial outcomes.

- Exercises to Enhance Persuasive Skills

1. Rewrite to Persuade

- Take a neutral statement and rewrite it to make it more persuasive.
- Neutral: *"This product helps with time management."* Persuasive: *"Master your time and unlock your potential with this innovative tool."*

2. Analyze Persuasive Speeches
Study famous speeches to identify techniques and vocabulary that make them compelling.
3. Craft a Call to Action
Write a short message encouraging someone to take a specific action.
Example:
"Join our cause today and be the change you wish to see."
To sum up, mastering the art of persuasive language is a valuable skill that extends across personal, professional, and societal domains. By understanding the psychological principles, employing strategic techniques, and adhering to ethical practices, you can use words to inspire, motivate, and influence others. Remember, the true power of persuasion lies not in manipulation but in fostering genuine connection and shared purpose.

CHAPTER SIXTEEN

Debunking Myths: Vocabulary for Unraveling Misconceptions

In a world teeming with information, myths and misconceptions find fertile ground to thrive. These false beliefs, often perpetuated by incomplete knowledge or emotional biases, can hinder progress, breed misunderstandings, and perpetuate societal problems. The antidote lies in the deliberate unraveling of these myths through precise and impactful communication. This chapter explores the vocabulary and techniques essential for debunking myths, enabling individuals to foster clarity, critical thinking, and informed discourse.

The Nature of Myths and Misconceptions

Myths are narratives that simplify complex realities, often blending facts with fiction. While they may offer comfort or explanations, they frequently diverge from truth, creating a distorted understanding.

Characteristics of Myths:

Emotional Appeal: Myths often evoke strong emotions, making them resistant to logic.

Cultural Embeddedness: Many myths are deeply rooted in cultural traditions and norms.

Resistance to Change: Myths persist due to cognitive biases, including the familiarity effect and confirmation bias.

Vocabulary for Debunking Myths

1. Clarifying Terms

Using precise language is critical for addressing misconceptions. Some effective clarifiers include:

"Misconception:" An incorrect belief or interpretation.

"Fallacy:" A flawed argument or reasoning.

"Assumption:" A belief taken for granted without proof.

Example:

"The common misconception that vaccines cause autism has been thoroughly debunked by scientific research."

2. Skeptical Phrases

Expressing doubt respectfully encourages critical examination.

"Let us examine the evidence."

"Is this claim supported by credible sources?"

3. Empirical Language

Words that emphasize evidence and research lend credibility.

"Data indicates," "Studies confirm," "Research reveals."

Example:

"Empirical data refutes the notion that intelligence is solely determined by genetics."

4. Analogies and Metaphors

Analogies simplify complex ideas, making them relatable.

"Believing in this myth is like navigating with a broken compass; it might feel right, but it leads you astray."

Strategies for Unraveling Misconceptions

1. Presenting Factual Evidence

Concrete evidence is the cornerstone of debunking myths.

Example:

"Contrary to the myth that humans use only 10% of their brains, neuroimaging studies show widespread activity across the brain."

2. Highlighting Logical Fallacies

Many myths persist due to flawed reasoning. Identifying these fallacies helps dismantle their credibility.

Common Fallacies:

"Post hoc ergo propter hoc" (after this, therefore because of this)

"Ad hominem" (attacking the person instead of the argument)

Example:

"The idea that climate change is a hoax because winters are still cold is a classic example of cherry-picking data."

3. Using Visual Aids

Charts, infographics, and comparisons can clarify complex data and challenge visual misconceptions.

4. Engaging in Dialogue

Respectful discussions encourage open-mindedness and foster understanding.

"Can we explore alternative perspectives on this topic?"

Vocabulary for Building Trust

1. Reassuring Phrases

Addressing emotional resistance with empathy fosters trust.

"I understand why this might seem plausible."

"It's natural to question unfamiliar concepts."

2. Encouraging Inquiry

Promote curiosity and critical thinking.

"What do you think could explain this phenomenon?"

"How can we verify this claim?"

3. Non-confrontational Phrases

Avoiding confrontational language maintains constructive conversations.

"Let's explore this further together."

"Can we delve into the evidence supporting this belief?"

Case Studies: Debunking Common Myths

1. The Flat Earth Myth

Myth: The Earth is flat. Reality: Centuries of astronomical observations and modern satellite imagery confirm the Earth's spherical shape. Approach:

Present scientific evidence, including images from space.

Highlight historical perspectives and advancements in navigation.

2. The "Natural Equals Safe" Fallacy

Myth: Natural products are always safe. Reality: Many natural substances, like arsenic, are harmful, while synthetic products often undergo rigorous safety testing. Approach:

Use examples to illustrate inconsistencies.

Discuss the role of regulation and testing in safety assurance.

3. The "We Only Use 10% of Our Brain" Myth

Myth: Humans use only 10% of their brain. Reality: Neuroimaging studies show extensive brain activity even during rest. Approach:

- Cite neuroscience research and experiments.
- Use analogies, such as comparing the brain to a city where all areas are interconnected.
- Building Resilience Against Myths

1. Promoting Media Literacy

Teaching individuals to critically evaluate sources and content can reduce susceptibility to myths.

2. Encouraging Scientific Literacy

Understanding the scientific method fosters appreciation for evidence-based conclusions.

3. Fostering Open-Mindedness

A willingness to question and revise beliefs is essential for overcoming misconceptions.

Exercises to Practice Debunking Myths

1. Analyze a Myth

Choose a widely held myth and identify its origins, why it persists, and how to counter it effectively.

2. Create a Persuasive Argument

Write a brief essay debunking a common misconception using evidence and persuasive language.

3. Role-Playing Debates

Engage in debates where one person defends a myth while the other dismantles it using facts.

Debunking myths is a vital skill in the information age. With the right vocabulary and strategies, individuals can challenge false beliefs, promote critical thinking, and foster a culture of informed decision-making. By addressing misconceptions respectfully and effectively, we pave the way for a more enlightened and rational society.

CHAPTER SEVENTEEN

Analyzing Arguments: Expressions for Critical Thinking and Evaluation

In a world where opinions abound and information is abundant, the ability to critically evaluate arguments is paramount. Analyzing arguments involves discerning the validity, relevance, and strength of claims, evidence, and reasoning. This chapter provides an in-depth exploration of the vocabulary and techniques essential for honing critical thinking skills and effectively evaluating arguments.

The Components of an Argument

Understanding the structure of arguments is the first step toward effective analysis. Most arguments consist of the following components:

- Claim: The main point or assertion.
- Evidence: The data, facts, or reasoning supporting the claim.
- Warrant: The connection between the evidence and the claim.
- Counterargument: Acknowledgment and rebuttal of opposing viewpoints.

Key Vocabulary for Argument Components:

- "Premise": A statement forming the basis of an argument.
- "Inference": A logical conclusion drawn from premises.
- "Conclusion": The end point or resolution of an argument.

Example:

"The premise that renewable energy reduces carbon emissions supports the conclusion that transitioning to green technologies is imperative."

Vocabulary for Critical Evaluation

1. Questioning Validity

To critically evaluate an argument, one must question its validity. Common expressions include:

"Does this claim follow logically from the evidence provided?"

"Are the premises sound and relevant?"

2. Assessing Evidence

Evaluating the quality and relevance of evidence is crucial. Useful phrases include:

"Is the evidence credible and well-sourced?"

"Does the data adequately support the argument?"

"How does this evidence compare to counter-evidence?"

3. Identifying Logical Fallacies

Logical fallacies undermine the strength of an argument. Common fallacies include:

"Straw man": Misrepresenting an opponent's argument to make it easier to attack.

"Red herring": Introducing irrelevant information to distract from the main issue.

"Slippery slope": Arguing that a minor action will inevitably lead to severe consequences.

Example:

"The argument relies on a slippery slope fallacy, suggesting that legalizing one drug will lead to the legalization of all drugs."

Techniques for Analyzing Arguments

1. Breaking Down Complex Arguments

Dissecting an argument into its components helps clarify its structure and assess its strength.

"Let's separate the claim from the supporting evidence to evaluate its coherence."

2. Comparative Analysis

Comparing arguments or perspectives reveals strengths, weaknesses, and biases.

"How does this viewpoint align with alternative perspectives?"

"What distinguishes this argument from opposing arguments?"

3. Evaluating Relevance

Relevance determines whether evidence and claims contribute meaningfully to the argument.

"Does this point directly address the issue at hand?"

4. Examining Assumptions

Many arguments rely on underlying assumptions, which may or may not be valid.

"What assumptions underlie this reasoning, and are they justified?"

Expressions for Supporting Critical Analysis

1. Agreement with Reservations

"While this argument is compelling, it overlooks certain key factors."

"I agree with the premise, but the evidence provided seems insufficient."

2. Polite Disagreement

"I'm not entirely convinced by this reasoning because..."

"This argument raises valid points but ultimately fails to address..."

3. Proposing Alternatives

"An alternative interpretation could be..."

"Have we considered the possibility that...?"

Advanced Techniques for Argument Analysis

1. Evaluating Causality

Arguments often claim causal relationships that require scrutiny.

"Does this evidence establish a direct causal link or merely a correlation?"

"Could there be other factors influencing the outcome?"

2. Assessing Ethical Implications

Some arguments have ethical dimensions that must be considered.

"What are the potential moral consequences of this action?"

"Does this argument align with widely accepted ethical principles?"

3. Cross-Disciplinary Perspectives

Integrating knowledge from various disciplines can provide a well-rounded evaluation.

"How does this argument hold up when viewed through the lens of sociology, economics, or psychology?"

Case Studies: Applying Critical Thinking

1. Debating Climate Change Policies

Claim: Carbon taxes reduce emissions. Evidence: Data from countries implementing carbon taxes shows reduced emissions over time. Counterargument: Critics argue carbon taxes disproportionately affect low-income households. Analysis:

- Assess the credibility of the data.
- Examine the fairness of the counterargument.

- Explore potential solutions, such as revenue recycling.

2. Evaluating Artificial Intelligence in Education

Claim: AI improves personalized learning. Evidence: Studies demonstrate that AI algorithms adapt to individual learning styles. Counterargument: AI lacks the empathy and creativity of human educators. Analysis:

- Compare benefits and limitations.
- Analyze the feasibility of integrating AI with traditional teaching.

3. Analyzing Media Bias

Claim: Media outlets often reflect political biases. Evidence: Studies show consistent framing differences in coverage of the same events. Counterargument: Some argue that bias is unavoidable and reflects societal diversity. Analysis:

- Investigate evidence supporting bias claims.
- Evaluate the argument's implications for media consumption and public trust.
- Developing a Critical Thinking Mindset

1. Curiosity and Open-Mindedness

Approach arguments with curiosity, seeking to understand rather than to refute.
"What can I learn from this perspective?"

2. Skeptical Inquiry

Adopt a healthy skepticism that questions assumptions and seeks evidence.
"What evidence supports this claim, and is it reliable?"

3. Collaborative Evaluation

Engage in discussions to test and refine arguments collaboratively.
"How might others interpret this evidence?"

4. Cultivating Analytical Rigor

Analytical rigor ensures a thorough and systematic evaluation of arguments.
"Have all relevant angles been considered?"
"What alternative explanations exist?"

Exercises for Practicing Argument Analysis

1. Argument Deconstruction

Choose a complex argument and break it into claims, evidence, and assumptions. Evaluate each component.

2. Logical Fallacy Identification

Analyze a debate or article to identify and critique logical fallacies.

3. Role-Playing Discussions

Engage in mock debates where participants defend or critique arguments using evidence-based reasoning.

4. Evidence Comparison

Gather evidence from multiple sources on a controversial topic. Compare the credibility, relevance, and implications of each source.

5. Hypothetical Scenarios

Create hypothetical arguments and challenge peers to evaluate them critically.

Analyzing arguments is a critical skill that empowers individuals to navigate a complex and information-rich world. By mastering the vocabulary and techniques for critical thinking, we can evaluate claims with precision, challenge fallacies effectively, and contribute to meaningful discussions. In doing so, we foster a culture of reasoned discourse and informed decision-making. Furthermore, developing a mindset of continuous learning and open inquiry ensures that our critical thinking skills remain sharp and adaptable in an ever-evolving intellectual landscape.

CHAPTER EIGHTEEN

The Power of Silence: Using Language Gaps to Create Impactful Moments

Silence, often overlooked in the cacophony of words, holds a profound power. It is a potent tool in communication, capable of creating space for reflection, emphasizing critical points, and fostering a deeper connection between individuals. Mastering the art of silence can transform mundane interactions into meaningful exchanges, providing a strategic edge in personal and professional life. This chapter explores the dynamics of silence, its psychological impact, and practical applications in various settings.

The Psychological Impact of Silence

Silence as a Cognitive Pause

Silence allows the brain to process information more effectively. In conversations, deliberate pauses give listeners time to absorb and reflect on what has been said. This cognitive break enhances comprehension and retention, ensuring that critical messages are not lost in the flow of dialogue.

Emotional Resonance

Silence can amplify emotions. A well-timed pause after a poignant statement can evoke introspection or a visceral response, leaving a lasting impression. This phenomenon is often utilized in storytelling, public speaking, and even negotiations to create a sense of gravitas.

The Tension of Anticipation

In certain contexts, silence generates anticipation. It compels the audience to focus, awaiting the next word or action. This deliberate withholding of information can heighten engagement and make the subsequent message more impactful.

Strategic Use of Silence in Communication

Building Rapport

Silence can foster a sense of trust and understanding. In active listening, remaining silent while someone speaks signals attentiveness and respect. This encourages openness and deepens interpersonal connections.

Highlighting Key Points

Pausing strategically before or after delivering crucial information emphasizes its importance. This technique is widely used in public speaking, where a brief silence can underscore a message's significance and ensure it resonates with the audience.

Managing Conflict

In conflict resolution, silence can diffuse tension. It allows all parties to cool down, gather their thoughts, and approach the discussion with a clearer perspective. Moreover, silence can serve as a non-confrontational way to assert boundaries or signal disagreement.

Negotiation Tactics

Silence is a powerful negotiation tool. When a proposal is met with silence, it often compels the other party to fill the gap, potentially revealing more information or making concessions. This subtle tactic can shift the balance of power in negotiations.

Silence in Professional Settings

Leadership and Authority

Leaders who use silence effectively exude confidence and control. Pausing before responding to questions or making decisions demonstrates thoughtfulness and decisiveness. It also encourages team members to voice their opinions, fostering a collaborative environment.

Enhancing Presentations

In presentations, silence can be used to pace the delivery, engage the audience, and highlight key points. For instance, pausing after a rhetorical question invites the audience to contemplate the answer, making the session more interactive and memorable.

Handling Difficult Conversations

Silence provides space for empathy in challenging discussions. Allowing moments of quiet can help the other person process their emotions and feel heard, paving the way for constructive dialogue.

Silence in Personal Relationships

Deepening Intimacy

In personal relationships, shared silence can be as meaningful as spoken words. It creates a sense of comfort and understanding, reflecting a deep connection that transcends verbal communication.

Resolving Misunderstandings

When emotions run high, silence can prevent impulsive reactions that might escalate the situation. It provides an opportunity to reflect, ensuring responses are thoughtful and measured.

Expressing Support

Sometimes, silence is the most profound way to show support. Being present without speaking allows individuals to feel acknowledged and comforted during moments of vulnerability.

Cultural Perspectives on Silence

Eastern Philosophies

In many Eastern cultures, silence is revered as a form of wisdom and self-control. Practices such as meditation and mindfulness emphasize the value of silence in achieving inner peace and clarity.

Western Communication Norms

In contrast, Western cultures often equate silence with discomfort or disengagement. However, its strategic use is gaining recognition in professional and personal contexts for its ability to enhance communication.

Bridging Cultural Differences

Understanding cultural attitudes toward silence is crucial in cross-cultural interactions. Being mindful of these differences can prevent misunderstandings and foster mutual respect.

Exercises for Mastering the Power of Silence

Reflective Listening

Engage in conversations where you consciously focus on listening without interrupting. Note how silence influences the flow and depth of the discussion.

Strategic Pausing

Practice incorporating deliberate pauses in your speech during presentations or meetings. Observe how it impacts the audience's engagement and comprehension.

Silent Observation

Spend time observing interactions without speaking. Reflect on the non-verbal cues and dynamics that silence brings to light.

Mindfulness Practice

Incorporate mindfulness exercises into your routine to become more comfortable with silence. This can enhance your ability to use it effectively in communication.

Silence Journaling

Document moments where silence made an impact in your day-to-day interactions. Reflect on what worked and what didn't, refining your ability to wield silence effectively.

Thus, the power of silence lies in its subtlety and versatility. It is a dynamic tool that can shape conversations, influence perceptions, and foster deeper connections. By embracing silence, we unlock a new dimension of communication—one that speaks volumes without uttering a single word. Mastering the art of silence is not just about refraining from speech but about using language gaps thoughtfully to create impactful moments that resonate deeply with others. As we cultivate this skill, we find that sometimes, the most profound messages are conveyed not through words but through the space between them.

CHAPTER NINETEEN

Elevating Conversations: Vocabulary for Engaging in Intellectual Discourse

In the pursuit of meaningful intellectual discourse, vocabulary serves as both a tool and a medium for communication. A rich vocabulary empowers individuals to articulate complex ideas, engage critically with diverse perspectives, and contribute effectively to academic and professional dialogues. Elevating conversations is not merely about using sophisticated words, but rather about employing a language that enhances clarity, fosters deep reflection, and challenges assumptions. This chapter delves into the significance of vocabulary in intellectual discourse, offering insights on how to harness language to stimulate and elevate conversations.

1. The Role of Vocabulary in Intellectual Discourse

Intellectual discourse encompasses a range of conversations, from philosophical debates to scientific discussions, from literary analysis to policy evaluations. The centrality of vocabulary in these interactions is undeniable, as it determines the effectiveness of communication. At its core, vocabulary in intellectual discourse goes beyond colloquial language; it involves the precise and intentional use of words that help convey nuanced meanings and promote deeper understanding.

1.1 Clarity and Precision

In intellectual conversations, the ability to express complex ideas clearly and precisely is paramount. Words are not simply carriers of meaning but vessels that encapsulate the very essence of thought. For example, the term "epistemology" refers to the study of knowledge, but its precise definition allows for deeper inquiries into how knowledge is constructed, validated, and understood. Using specialized terminology such as this enriches the conversation, making it more effective and focused on the topic at hand.

1.2 Critical Thinking and Reflection

A well-developed vocabulary invites individuals to think critically about their ideas and the perspectives of others. Terms such as "dialectical," "heuristics," and "paradigms" are more than just jargon; they encourage reflective thinking. These words push participants to consider the origins, structures, and implications of their arguments, fostering deeper engagement with the material.

1.3 The Ability to Challenge Assumptions

In intellectual discourse, vocabulary serves as a means to challenge the status quo. Words like "reification," "ideology," and "hegemony" allow participants to dissect and critique assumptions that are often left unquestioned. Such terms provide the tools to engage with entrenched ideas and offer alternative frameworks for understanding the world.

2. Building a Robust Vocabulary for Intellectual Discourse

A strong vocabulary is not something that can be built overnight; it is cultivated through reading, exposure to diverse subjects, and active engagement with the intellectual community. Here are some strategies for developing a vocabulary that enhances intellectual discourse:

2.1 Engage with Classic and Contemporary Texts

To develop a rich vocabulary, it is essential to engage with both classic and contemporary works across various disciplines. Reading texts from different fields—such as philosophy, history, literature, and social sciences—exposes one to diverse lexicons and intellectual frameworks. Key works such as Plato's "Republic," Foucault's "Discipline and Punish," and Marx's "Das Kapital" offer a wealth of specialized terminology that helps readers understand and articulate complex ideas.

2.2 Study Specialized Terminology

Certain fields have their own jargon and specialized vocabulary. For instance, in law, terms like "precedent," "stare decisis," and "jurisprudence" are crucial for understanding legal arguments. In science, terms such as "hypothesis," "correlation," and "empirical data" facilitate precise communication. A concerted effort to study these terms enhances one's ability to navigate intellectual discourse in specific domains.

2.3 Practice Using New Vocabulary

Simply learning new words is not enough; they must be actively incorporated into one's speech and writing. Regularly using new vocabulary in conversations and academic papers is essential for solidifying understanding. This can be done by writing essays, engaging in discussions, or presenting ideas in public forums. The more one practices, the more naturally these words will come to mind when needed.

2.4 Engage with Diverse Perspectives

To truly elevate conversations, it is important to engage with diverse perspectives and learn the vocabulary that accompanies them. This includes understanding different cultural, philosophical, and intellectual traditions. A global perspective allows individuals to use vocabulary that resonates across cultural boundaries, making conversations richer and more inclusive.

3. Key Vocabulary for Intellectual Discourse

The vocabulary used in intellectual discourse must be varied and multifaceted. Below are several categories of vocabulary that are essential for elevating conversations:

3.1 Philosophical and Theoretical Vocabulary

Philosophical discussions often rely on terms that delve into the very nature of knowledge, existence, and reality. Words like "ontology," "epistemology," and "metaphysics" are foundational in discussions about the nature of being and knowing. These terms allow participants to probe into the depths of fundamental concepts.

Ontology: The study of being and existence.

- Epistemology: The theory of knowledge, especially with regard to its methods, validity, and scope.
- Metaphysics: A branch of philosophy that deals with the first principles of things, including abstract concepts such as being, knowing, cause, identity, time, and space.

3.2 Rhetorical and Argumentative Vocabulary

In intellectual discourse, the ability to argue effectively is essential. Vocabulary related to rhetoric, logic, and argumentation plays a critical role in ensuring that conversations remain coherent and well-structured. Terms like "syllogism," "fallacy," "antithesis," and "rhetorical appeals" are fundamental in making logical arguments and identifying flawed reasoning.

- Syllogism: A form of reasoning in which a conclusion is drawn from two given or assumed propositions (premises).
- Fallacy: A mistaken belief, especially one based on unsound arguments.
- Antithesis: A rhetorical device in which two opposite ideas are put together in a sentence to achieve a contrasting effect.

3.3 Scientific and Analytical Vocabulary

Intellectual discourse often ventures into scientific discussions, where precise language is necessary for conveying data, observations, and conclusions. Terms like "methodology," "empirical evidence," and "hypothesis" allow participants to describe research processes and outcomes accurately.

- Methodology: A system of methods used in a particular area of study or activity.

- Empirical Evidence: Information acquired by observation or experimentation.
- Hypothesis: A proposed explanation made on the basis of limited evidence as a starting point for further investigation.

3.4 Political and Social Vocabulary

In discussions about politics and society, a nuanced understanding of terminology is crucial for addressing issues such as power, justice, and equity. Terms like "hegemony," "intersectionality," and "neoliberalism" are frequently used to analyze societal structures and their impact on different groups.

- Hegemony: Leadership or dominance, especially by one country or social group over others.
- Intersectionality: The interconnected nature of social categorizations such as race, class, and gender, which create overlapping and interdependent systems of discrimination or disadvantage.
- Neoliberalism: A political approach that favors free-market capitalism, deregulation, and a reduction in government spending.

3.5 Literary and Artistic Vocabulary

In the realm of literature and the arts, vocabulary is essential for discussing themes, techniques, and interpretations. Terms like "metaphor," "allusion," and "allegory" help participants delve into the subtleties of artistic expression.

- Metaphor: A figure of speech in which a word or phrase is applied to an object or action to which it is not literally applicable.
- Allusion: An expression designed to call something to mind without mentioning it explicitly.
- Allegory: A narrative in which characters and events represent abstract ideas or moral qualities.

4. The Impact of Vocabulary on Social and Cultural Dialogue

Elevating conversations through vocabulary is not just an intellectual exercise—it has profound social and cultural implications. Effective vocabulary can bridge gaps between different worldviews, promote empathy, and foster inclusive discussions.

4.1 Inclusive Language and Respectful Discourse

Using inclusive language is essential for ensuring that intellectual discourse is respectful and considers diverse experiences. Terms like "equity," "empowerment," and "representation" are crucial in discussions surrounding social justice and human rights. A vocabulary that embraces inclusivity and respect for all individuals, regardless of their background or identity, is foundational for promoting healthy dialogue.

4.2 Facilitating Cross-Cultural Communication

In a globalized world, vocabulary plays a key role in fostering cross-cultural understanding. Understanding the terminology of different cultures, histories, and traditions allows for more productive and respectful exchanges between individuals from diverse backgrounds. It promotes awareness and sensitivity, essential components of intellectual discourse in an interconnected world.

A well-rounded and refined vocabulary is indispensable for engaging in intellectual discourse. It not only facilitates clear and effective communication but also enhances critical thinking, reflection, and the ability to challenge assumptions. By expanding one's vocabulary across various fields—philosophy, rhetoric, science, politics, and the arts—individuals can contribute to more meaningful, elevated conversations that push the boundaries of knowledge and understanding. Ultimately, the richness of our vocabulary shapes the depth and quality of our intellectual engagements, making it a powerful tool for both personal and societal transformation.

A well-rounded and refined vocabulary is indispensable for engaging in intellectual discourse. It not only facilitates clear and effective communication but also enhances critical thinking, reflection, and the ability to challenge assumptions. By expanding one's vocabulary across various fields—philosophy, rhetoric, science, politics, and the arts—individuals can contribute to more meaningful, elevated conversations that push the boundaries of knowledge and understanding. Ultimately, the richness of our vocabulary shapes the depth and quality of our intellectual engagements, making it a powerful tool for both personal and societal transformation.

CHAPTER TWENTY

Becoming a Master Wordsmith: Strategies for Expanding Your Vocabulary Continuously

Language is the cornerstone of human communication, and a rich vocabulary is its most valuable asset. Being a master wordsmith means having the ability to wield words with precision, creativity, and impact. Whether you're an academic, a professional, or simply a lover of language, continuously expanding your vocabulary is a lifelong journey that enriches both personal expression and intellectual engagement. This chapter explores effective strategies for cultivating a dynamic vocabulary and provides practical tools for incorporating new words into everyday use.

1. The Importance of Vocabulary Mastery

Vocabulary is more than just a collection of words; it shapes how we think, express ourselves, and interact with the world. A strong vocabulary enhances communication, boosts confidence, and opens the door to opportunities across various domains.

1.1 The Cognitive Benefits

Expanding your vocabulary improves cognitive functions such as memory, comprehension, and critical thinking. Studies show that individuals with a robust vocabulary are better equipped to process complex ideas, solve problems, and engage in abstract reasoning.

1.2 Enhanced Communication Skills

Mastery of words allows for precise and impactful expression. It enables individuals to articulate their thoughts clearly, avoid misunderstandings, and leave lasting impressions in both personal and professional contexts.

1.3 Cultural and Social Empowerment

Vocabulary also serves as a bridge between cultures and communities. Understanding and using diverse words allows for deeper engagement with literature, art, and social issues, fostering empathy and global awareness.

2. Strategies for Expanding Your Vocabulary

Building a rich vocabulary is an intentional and iterative process. The following strategies provide a comprehensive approach to becoming a master wordsmith.

2.1 Read Widely and Regularly

Reading is one of the most effective ways to encounter new words. By immersing yourself in diverse texts, you naturally expand your vocabulary while gaining context for how words are used.

Explore Different Genres: Read novels, essays, scientific articles, and poetry to encounter a broad spectrum of words.

Incorporate Challenging Material: Push yourself to read texts slightly above your current comprehension level to encounter unfamiliar terms.

2.2 Keep a Vocabulary Journal

Documenting new words is essential for retention. A dedicated journal allows you to track, review, and incorporate words into your repertoire.

Write Definitions and Examples: Note the meaning of each new word and how it is used in a sentence.

Add Synonyms and Antonyms: Expand your understanding of each word by learning related terms.

2.3 Use Flashcards and Spaced Repetition

Flashcards are a practical tool for memorizing vocabulary. Pair them with spaced repetition software (SRS) like Anki or Quizlet to optimize retention.

Create Digital or Physical Flashcards: Write the word on one side and its definition, usage, and synonyms on the other.

Review Periodically: Revisit cards at increasing intervals to reinforce memory.

2.4 Engage in Active Practice

- Active use of new words is crucial for mastering them. Practice integrating vocabulary into your speech and writing.
- Challenge Yourself to Use New Words Daily: Set a goal to use a certain number of new words in conversations or emails.
- Write Short Stories or Essays: Use creative writing as a way to experiment with and reinforce new vocabulary.

2.5 Play Word Games and Puzzles

Games like Scrabble, Boggle, and crosswords are entertaining and educational. They expose you to new words while sharpening your language skills.

- Try Vocabulary Apps: Platforms like WordUp, Vocabulary.com, and Duolingo provide interactive ways to learn new words.
- Join Wordsmith Communities: Engage with groups that share a love for language and wordplay.

2.6 Learn Roots, Prefixes, and Suffixes

- Understanding the building blocks of words can help you decipher unfamiliar terms and predict their meanings.
- Study Latin and Greek Roots: Many English words have origins in these languages. For example, "bio" (life) and "logy" (study) combine to form "biology."
- Recognize Common Prefixes and Suffixes: Prefixes like "un-" (not) and suffixes like "-able" (capable of) provide clues to a word's meaning.

2.7 Expose Yourself to Other Languages

- Learning a new language not only expands your vocabulary in that language but also deepens your understanding of English.
- Borrowed Words: English has absorbed words from languages like French, German, and Japanese (e.g., "genre," "kindergarten," "tsunami").
- Cognates: Recognizing similar words across languages can expand your lexicon.

2.8 Watch and Listen Intentionally

- Consume media with the goal of learning. Pay attention to the language used in documentaries, podcasts, and speeches.
- Use Subtitles: Watching movies or shows with subtitles helps link pronunciation with spelling and meaning.
- Listen to Audiobooks: Hearing words in context improves both comprehension and pronunciation.

3. Overcoming Challenges in Vocabulary Expansion

While expanding your vocabulary is rewarding, it can also be challenging. Addressing these obstacles ensures consistent progress.

3.1 Retention Difficulties

To combat forgetting, reinforce your learning through repetition and active usage. Create associations or mnemonic devices to anchor words in memory.

3.2 Overwhelming Quantity

Focus on quality over quantity. Learn a manageable number of words at a time, and ensure deep understanding rather than superficial memorization.

3.3 Lack of Motivation

Set specific goals, such as mastering 10 new words per week. Celebrate milestones to maintain enthusiasm.

4. Incorporating Vocabulary into Everyday Life

To truly master vocabulary, make it a part of your daily routine. Consistency is key to turning new words into permanent tools.

4.1 Engage in Intellectual Conversations

Discussing topics that interest you is a natural way to practice and reinforce new words. Join book clubs, debate groups, or online forums.

4.2 Teach Others

Explaining new words to friends, students, or colleagues helps solidify your understanding and makes learning collaborative.

4.3 Use Technology

Leverage apps, websites, and digital tools to integrate vocabulary practice into your daily life. Many platforms gamify the process, making it enjoyable.

4.4 Personalize Your Learning

Tailor your vocabulary-building efforts to align with your interests, career goals, or hobbies. This makes the process relevant and meaningful.

5. Measuring Progress as a Wordsmith

Tracking your progress is essential for maintaining momentum and refining your approach.

5.1 Set Milestones

Define clear, achievable goals, such as learning 500 words in six months. Break these goals into smaller, weekly or monthly targets.

5.2 Test Yourself

Periodically assess your vocabulary through quizzes, writing exercises, or word games. Note areas for improvement.

5.3 Celebrate Growth

Recognize how your expanded vocabulary improves your communication and confidence. Reflect on how far you've come in your journey as a wordsmith.

Thus, becoming a master wordsmith is a lifelong endeavor that requires curiosity, discipline, and creativity. By employing the strategies outlined in this chapter—reading widely, practicing actively, and engaging with language in diverse ways—you can continuously expand your vocabulary and enrich your personal and professional life. Mastery of words is not just about knowing more; it's about using language to connect, inspire, and transform.

CHAPTER TWENTY-ONE

Power-packed phrases/chunks

Language is not just about individual words; it is about how they come together to create meaning, evoke emotions, and convey complex ideas. Power-packed phrases or "chunks" are pre-assembled blocks of language that allow speakers and writers to communicate with clarity, creativity, and persuasion. These phrases transcend the literal meaning of individual words, adding layers of nuance and impact. Mastering the use of such chunks can elevate your communication skills to new heights, making your language more engaging and memorable.

This chapter delves into the concept of power-packed phrases, their role in communication, and practical strategies to incorporate them into everyday conversations, speeches, and writing.

1. What Are Power-Packed Phrases?

Power-packed phrases are groups of words that work together to express a single idea or evoke a specific response. They are memorable, impactful, and often carry cultural, emotional, or rhetorical significance.

1.1 Characteristics of Power-Packed Phrases

- Conciseness: These phrases pack a punch in a few words, saving time while delivering maximum effect.
- Clarity: They are easy to understand and resonate with diverse audiences.
- Cultural Resonance: Many power-packed phrases draw from literature, history, or common idiomatic expressions, making them relatable.

1.2 Examples in Everyday Use

"Break the ice" – To initiate a conversation in an awkward situation.
"The tip of the iceberg" – Indicating a small part of a much larger issue.
"Think outside the box" – Encouraging creative or unconventional thinking.

2. Why Are Phrases and Chunks So Powerful?

2.1 Streamlining Communication

Chunks allow for the rapid transmission of complex ideas without requiring lengthy explanations. For example, "time is money" succinctly conveys the value of time.

2.2 Enhancing Memorability

Phrases like "all that glitters is not gold" stick in the audience's mind because of their rhythm, rhyme, or metaphorical depth.

2.3 Creating Emotional Connections

Words grouped in powerful phrases often evoke emotions, whether it's inspiration ("carpe diem"), encouragement ("keep the faith"), or caution ("better safe than sorry").

2.4 Building Credibility

Using well-known phrases can lend authority to your communication by aligning your ideas with universally understood concepts.

3. Types of Power-Packed Phrases

3.1 Idiomatic Expressions

Definition: These are figurative phrases that convey meanings beyond the literal interpretation of the words.
Examples:

"Bite the bullet" – To face a difficult situation with courage.
"Spill the beans" – To reveal a secret.

3.2 Proverbs and Sayings

Definition: These are traditional phrases encapsulating wisdom or universal truths.

Examples:

"Actions speak louder than words."

"A stitch in time saves nine."

3.3 Metaphors and Similes

Definition: Figurative language used to compare concepts creatively.

Examples:

"As quiet as a mouse."

"Life is a rollercoaster."

3.4 Rhetorical Devices

Definition: Phrases designed to persuade or emphasize a point.

Examples:

"We shall overcome."

"Ask not what your country can do for you; ask what you can do for your country."

3.5 Corporate Jargon and Buzzwords

Definition: Phrases commonly used in professional and organizational settings.

Examples:

"Leverage your strengths."

"Raise the bar."

4. Incorporating Power-Packed Phrases into Your Communication

4.1 Know Your Audience

Select phrases that resonate with your audience's cultural background, experiences, and expectations.

4.2 Practice Contextual Usage

Using a phrase inappropriately can confuse or alienate your audience. Ensure the chosen chunk aligns with the topic and tone.

Example of misuse: Using "raining cats and dogs" in a formal weather report.

Correct use: "The downpour was so heavy, it was like it was raining cats and dogs."

4.3 Enhance Originality

While borrowing phrases, aim to personalize or adapt them for originality.

Instead of: "The ball is in your court."

Try: "The decision is entirely yours now."

4.4 Blend Phrases Seamlessly

Avoid overloading your speech or writing with too many power-packed phrases, as it may come off as artificial or pretentious.

5. Learning and Mastering Chunks

5.1 Read and Observe

Expose yourself to diverse texts—literature, speeches, and media—to identify commonly used phrases.

5.2 Maintain a Phrase Bank

Keep a journal or digital list of impactful phrases, noting their meanings and examples of usage.

5.3 Practice Regularly

Integrate new phrases into your daily communication through conversations, emails, or essays.

5.4 Engage in Active Listening

Pay attention to the language used in interviews, podcasts, and presentations. Observe how speakers use chunks to convey their points.

5.5 Use Language Tools

Apps and resources like idiom dictionaries or vocabulary builders can help you discover and practice power-packed phrases.

6. Examples of Power-Packed Phrases in Action

6.1 In Speeches

"The only thing we have to fear is fear itself." – Franklin D. Roosevelt

"I have a dream." – Martin Luther King Jr.

6.2 In Marketing

"Just do it." – Nike

"Because you're worth it." – L'Oréal

6.3 In Literature

"It was the best of times, it was the worst of times." – Charles Dickens

"To be or not to be, that is the question." – William Shakespeare

6.4 In Everyday Life

"No pain, no gain."

"What doesn't kill you makes you stronger."

7. Avoiding Overuse and Misuse

7.1 Know When Less Is More

Using too many power-packed phrases can dilute their impact. Be selective and strategic.

7.2 Beware of Clichés

While some phrases are universally appealing, others may feel overused or outdated.

Overused: "At the end of the day."

Better alternative: "Ultimately."

7.3 Understand Nuances

Ensure you grasp the cultural or situational nuances of a phrase before using it.

Conclusion

Power-packed phrases are the unsung heroes of impactful communication. By mastering the art of using chunks, you can enrich your language, captivate your audience, and make your messages unforgettable. However, like any tool, these phrases must be used with precision, purpose, and authenticity. As you explore and experiment with this linguistic treasure chest, you will find yourself not only communicating more effectively but also connecting more deeply with those around you.

Elevate your language with the power of well-crafted phrases, and let your words leave a lasting impression!

Exercises

Exercise 1: Identifying Key Themes

Based on the excerpts and concepts provided, identify the primary themes discussed in the text. Write a brief paragraph summarizing each theme, focusing on how they relate to human behavior, leadership, and societal structures.

Exercise 2: Rephrasing for Clarity and Impact

Select five sentences or phrases from the provided text and rewrite them to enhance clarity and impact. For example:

Original: "He poured out his hot wrath upon him calling him a curse on the nation."

Rephrased: "He unleashed his fury, condemning him as a curse upon the nation."

Exercise 3: Contextual Analysis

Choose three power-packed phrases or sentences from the text and analyze their context. Discuss what they imply about the speaker's mindset, the societal framework, or the intended audience.

Exercise 4: Creating Analogies

Using the text as inspiration, create three analogies or metaphors that align with the themes of perseverance, human connection, or ambition. For example:

"Life wrecked all her dream ships on the sharp rocks of reality" could inspire:

"Her ambitions crumbled like a sandcastle against the rising tide of adversity."

Exercise 5: Cooperative Vision

Reflect on the question, "Can you name one cooperative that has swelled in size and become a really effective operation?" Research and present an example of such a cooperative, detailing its growth, impact, and lessons it offers for collective human effort.

Exercise 6: Building Sentences

Using these phrases as prompts, construct meaningful sentences that highlight their significance:

"A stifling wave of remorse swept over me."

"History sparkles with amusing examples of..."

"There is only one way under high heaven."

Exercise 7: Inspirational Writing

Write a short motivational paragraph using at least three of the following phrases:

"Life blasted all her hopes."

"God had set blooming your heart."

"A flaming urge with a feeling of importance."

Exercise 8: Comparative Study

Compare the stylistic elements of the provided text with another work of motivational or reflective writing. Identify similarities and differences in tone, language, and message delivery.

Exercise 9: Phrase-to-Action Conversion

Select three power-packed phrases from the text and describe how they can be turned into actionable advice or practices in real-life scenarios. For example:

Phrase: *"Consulting students about their wishes and desires was just the shot in the arm for them."*

Action: *"Regularly seek feedback from your team to boost morale and productivity."*

Exercise 10: Creating a Vision Statement

Using the themes and phrases from the text, draft a vision statement for a cooperative or organization that embodies collective progress, resilience, and innovation.

These exercises aim to engage readers in critical thinking, creativity, and practical application, fostering a deeper understanding of the powerful messages within the text.

Collocation Practice

Collocations are combinations of words that naturally go together in English. Learning collocations helps you sound more fluent and confident because native speakers use these word combinations instinctively. This chapter provides an introduction to collocations, their types, and exercises to practice them.

1. What Are Collocations?

A collocation is a pair or group of words that are often used together. For example:

Make a decision (correct) vs. Do a decision (incorrect)

Fast car (correct) vs. Quick car (incorrect)

Using the correct collocations improves both your spoken and written English.

2. Types of Collocations

Collocations can be categorized into several types:

2.1 Adjective + Noun

Example: strong coffee, heavy rain, deep regret

2.2 Verb + Noun

Example: make a mistake, take a break, give advice

2.3 Noun + Noun

Example: traffic jam, wedding ceremony, human rights

2.4 Adverb + Adjective

Example: highly successful, deeply disappointed, completely different

2.5 Verb + Preposition

Example: rely on, agree with, focus on

2.6 Preposition + Noun

Example: in advance, at risk, on purpose

3. Why Are Collocations Important?

They make your language sound natural.

They help with effective communication.

They enhance fluency and understanding in conversations and writing.

4. Exercises on Collocations

Exercise 1: Match the Collocations

Match the words in Column A with their correct pairs in Column B:

Column A Column B

Make a decision

Heavy rain

Fast car

Deeply disappointed

Take a break

Exercise 2: Fill-in-the-Blanks

Complete the sentences with the correct collocations:

- I need to _______ a decision about my career soon. (make/do)
- The weather forecast predicted _______ rain tomorrow. (heavy/strong)
- She was _______ disappointed when she didn't get the job. (deeply/highly)
- Can you _______ me a favor and help with this task? (do/make)
- We should _______ a break before continuing our work. (take/have)

Exercise 3: Identify Incorrect Collocations

Find and correct the incorrect collocations in the sentences:

- He gave a mistake during the exam.
- I took a big decision yesterday.
- She had a quick car that everyone admired.
- The teacher was highly angered by the students.
- They focused in completing the project on time.

Exercise 4: Create Your Own Sentences
Use the given collocations in sentences of your own:
Pay attention
Break a promise
Strong argument
Run a business
Do homework
5. Common Collocations List
Adjective + Noun
Bright future
Common mistake
Strong possibility
Verb + Noun
Make progress
Catch a bus
Give a speech
Adverb + Adjective
Highly effective
Seriously injured
Deeply grateful
6. Tips for Learning Collocations
Read and Listen Regularly: Notice how words are paired in books, articles, and conversations.
Use Flashcards: Write collocations on flashcards and review them daily.
Practice in Context: Always try to use collocations in sentences to understand their meaning and usage.
Group Collocations by Topic: Learn collocations related to specific themes like travel, work, or education.

By mastering collocations, you will not only expand your vocabulary but also make your English sound more natural and fluent. Keep practicing!

Powerful Chunks From Newspapers

Below is an expanded collection of impactful phrases, or "chunks," drawn from newspapers across various domains, enriched with explanations and illustrative examples.

Politics and Governance

"Unprecedented backlash over..."

Explanation: Used to describe intense opposition or criticism, often in response to policies or decisions by authorities.

Example: "The government faced *unprecedented backlash over* its decision to reduce public healthcare funding, sparking protests nationwide."

"A turning point in the legislative debate."

Explanation: Signifies a crucial moment that changes the direction of discussions on a law or policy.

Example: "The opposition's compelling arguments *marked a turning point in the legislative debate* on data privacy laws."

"Swift measures to address the mounting crisis."

Explanation: Highlights rapid actions taken to mitigate an escalating problem.

Example: "*Swift measures, including a nationwide lockdown, were implemented to address the mounting crisis of the pandemic.*"

"Echoes of dissent resound across the chambers."

Explanation: Reflects widespread disagreement within political or legislative assemblies.

Example: "During the parliamentary session, *echoes of dissent resounded across the chambers as lawmakers debated the contentious bill.*"

"A landmark verdict that reshapes the legal landscape."

Explanation: Describes a court decision with far-reaching implications.

Example: "The Supreme Court's ruling on environmental laws is a *landmark verdict that reshapes the legal landscape.*"

Economics and Finance

"Markets react sharply to policy announcements."

Explanation: Indicates volatility in financial markets following major policy declarations.

Example: "*Markets reacted sharply to the central bank's announcement* of interest rate hikes, with stocks plunging by 3%."

"Investors brace for volatility amidst geopolitical tensions."

Explanation: Depicts a cautious outlook among investors during uncertain political situations.

Example: "As tensions escalated in the Middle East, investors braced for volatility, moving towards safer assets like gold."

"Inflation concerns loom over the economic forecast."

Explanation: Highlights the pervasive worry about rising prices impacting the economy.

Example: "Inflation concerns loom over the economic forecast as fuel prices hit a 10-year high."

"A rally driven by renewed optimism."

Explanation: Describes a surge in financial markets driven by positive sentiment.

Example: "Stock markets witnessed a rally driven by renewed optimism over the signing of a trade deal."

"Fiscal strategies to cushion the downturn."

Explanation: Refers to economic policies designed to mitigate the effects of a recession.

Example: "The government unveiled fiscal strategies to cushion the downturn, including tax relief and increased public spending."

Environment and Climate Change

"Rising sea levels threaten coastal communities."

Explanation: Draws attention to the impact of climate change on populations near oceans.

Example: "Rising sea levels, caused by melting polar ice, threaten coastal communities across the Pacific Islands."

"A global pact to combat deforestation."

Explanation: Indicates international agreements aimed at preserving forests.

Example: "Countries signed a global pact to combat deforestation, pledging to plant 1 billion trees by 2030."

"Urgent calls for sustainable energy solutions."

Explanation: Reflects the demand for eco-friendly energy alternatives.

Example: "Amid increasing carbon emissions, urgent calls for sustainable energy solutions dominated the climate summit."

"Alarming trends in greenhouse gas emissions."

Explanation: Highlights the concerning rise in pollutants contributing to global warming.

Example: "The report revealed alarming trends in greenhouse gas emissions, urging immediate action to curb industrial output."

"Wildlife on the brink amid habitat destruction."

Explanation: Depicts the dire situation faced by animal species due to loss of natural habitats.

Example: "Wildlife, including endangered tigers, is on the brink amid habitat destruction caused by illegal logging."

Science and Technology

"Revolutionizing industries through AI breakthroughs."

Explanation: Describes transformative changes across sectors due to advancements in artificial intelligence.

Example: "AI breakthroughs are revolutionizing industries, from healthcare to manufacturing, with automated solutions."

"The space race intensifies with new players."

Explanation: Reflects the growing competition among nations and private entities in space exploration.

Example: "The space race intensifies with new players like India and private companies entering lunar exploration missions."

"Breakthrough discovery in renewable energy."

Explanation: Highlights a significant finding that advances sustainable energy production.

Example: "Scientists announced a breakthrough discovery in renewable energy, making solar cells 50% more efficient."

"Ethical dilemmas in the age of biotechnology."

Explanation: Discusses the moral challenges posed by advancements in genetics and related fields.

Example: "The cloning of endangered species sparks ethical dilemmas in the age of biotechnology."

"Cybersecurity threats pose a challenge to global stability."

Explanation: Points to the risks posed by cyberattacks to international peace and security.

Example: "Recent ransomware attacks highlight how cybersecurity threats pose a challenge to global stability."

Social and Cultural

"A cultural renaissance reshaping artistic expression."

Explanation: Describes a revival or flourishing of creativity in arts and culture.

Example: "A cultural renaissance reshaping artistic expression is taking hold, blending traditional art with modern technology."

"A society grappling with the challenges of inclusivity."

Explanation: Reflects the ongoing struggle to achieve diversity and equality in social structures.

Example: "A society grappling with the challenges of inclusivity faces heated debates over affirmative action policies."

"The silent struggles of mental health awareness."

Explanation: Discusses the often-overlooked issues related to mental health.

Example: "Despite growing campaigns, the silent struggles of mental health awareness remain pervasive in workplaces."

"A generation redefining work-life balance."

Explanation: Describes the evolving priorities of younger demographics towards balancing career and personal life.

Example: "With remote work becoming a norm, a generation is redefining work-life balance in unprecedented ways."

"Traditions under threat in a rapidly modernizing world."

Explanation: Highlights the pressures on cultural traditions due to modernization.

Example: "Festivals and rituals are traditions under threat in a rapidly modernizing world."

Sports and Entertainment

"A stunning comeback that defied all odds."

Explanation: Describes a dramatic reversal of fortune in sports or performance.

Example: "The team's stunning comeback that defied all odds secured their place in the finals."

"Breaking barriers in a male-dominated industry."

Explanation: Highlights achievements by women or marginalized groups in traditionally male-dominated fields.

Example: "The director broke barriers in a male-dominated industry, becoming the first woman to win this prestigious award."

"A cinematic masterpiece that resonates with audiences."

Explanation: Praises a film for its emotional or intellectual impact.

Example: "The film has been hailed as a cinematic masterpiece that resonates with audiences worldwide."

"Records shattered in an unforgettable performance."

Explanation: Describes extraordinary achievements in sports or entertainment.

Example: "The sprinter shattered records in an unforgettable performance at the Olympics."

"The unrelenting pursuit of athletic excellence."

Explanation: Reflects the dedication and hard work of athletes striving for greatness.

Example: "Her unrelenting pursuit of athletic excellence has made her a role model for young athletes."

These expanded examples and explanations provide a comprehensive understanding of how powerful chunks can be utilized effectively in various contexts. For exercises, refer to the previous section and incorporate these phrases in creative and analytical writing tasks.

Innovative Ways For Boosting Your English Vocabulary

There are some innovative and creative ways to boost your English vocabulary:

1. Storyboarding

Create a Storyboard: Choose a set of new words and create a storyboard or comic strip. Write a short story using the new words and draw accompanying illustrations.

Visual Aid: Visual aids can help in better retention and understanding of new vocabulary.

2. Vocabulary Videos

Create Videos: Make short videos or vlogs where you use new words in context. Explain the meaning and usage of the words.

Share and Collaborate: Share your videos with friends or online communities and ask for feedback.

3. Word Association Games

Mind Maps: Create mind maps linking new words to related words, synonyms, and antonyms.

Association Chains: Start with one word and see how many related words you can come up with. For example, "happy" -> "joyful" -> "ecstatic" -> "thrilled".

4. Language Exchange Partners

Find a Partner: Pair up with a language exchange partner who is a native English speaker.

Practice Conversations: Engage in regular conversations and focus on using new vocabulary words.

5. Flash Fiction Writing

Flash Fiction: Write very short stories (100-500 words) using a set list of new vocabulary words.

Creative Writing: This exercise helps in using new words creatively and contextually.

6. Interactive Apps and Games

Apps: Use language learning apps like Duolingo, Memrise, or Babbel which incorporate gamification to make learning fun.

Online Games: Play online vocabulary games and quizzes to reinforce learning.

7. Vocabulary Challenges

Weekly Challenges: Set weekly vocabulary challenges for yourself and your friends. For example, learn 10 new words and use each of them in a sentence.

Reward System: Create a reward system to motivate yourself to achieve your vocabulary goals.

8. Book Club with a Twist

Themed Book Club: Start or join a book club where the focus is on learning and discussing new vocabulary words from the book.

Vocabulary Discussions: During discussions, highlight and explore new words and their meanings.

9. Engage with Multilingual Content

Translations: Read translations of books or articles in your native language and English to compare and understand new words.

Subtitled Media: Watch movies or shows with subtitles to see how new words are used in different contexts.

10. Word Puzzles and Crosswords

Create Puzzles: Design your own crossword puzzles or word searches using new vocabulary words.

Solve Puzzles: Regularly solving word puzzles can significantly enhance your vocabulary.

11. Social Media Interaction

Follow Language Accounts: Follow social media accounts and pages dedicated to English vocabulary building.

Daily Words: Participate in daily word challenges and quizzes posted by these accounts.

12. Digital Flashcards

Create Flashcards: Use digital flashcard apps like Anki or Quizlet to create flashcards with new words, definitions, and example sentences.

Review Regularly: Regularly review the flashcards to reinforce your memory.

13. Podcast and Audiobook Integration

Listen Actively: Choose podcasts and audiobooks that interest you and actively listen for new words.

Note-Taking: Take notes of new words and try to use them in sentences later.

14. Interactive Workshops and Webinars

Join Workshops: Participate in interactive language workshops and webinars focused on vocabulary building.

Interactive Learning: Engage in activities and exercises during these sessions to practice new words.

15. Role-Playing Activities

Role-Playing Games: Engage in role-playing games (RPGs) where you can practice using new vocabulary in various scenarios.

Scenario Creation: Create different scenarios and dialogues using new words to practice contextually.

By incorporating these innovative and engaging methods into your routine, you'll find vocabulary building to be an enjoyable and rewarding experience. Happy learning!

Ultramodern Ways For Boosting Vocabulary

Here are some ultramodern and cutting-edge ways to boost your vocabulary:

1. Virtual Reality (VR) Language Immersion

VR Experiences: Use VR platforms to immerse yourself in a virtual environment where you can practice language skills.

Interactive Learning: Engage in conversations with virtual characters or explore virtual worlds where you need to use new vocabulary words.

2. AI Language Tutors

AI Apps: Use AI-powered language learning apps that provide personalized vocabulary lessons and feedback.

Chatbots: Interact with AI chatbots designed to help you practice and learn new words in real-time.

3. Augmented Reality (AR) Flashcards

AR Flashcards: Utilize AR apps that bring flashcards to life by displaying 3D images and animations associated with new vocabulary words.

Interactive Learning: Scan objects around you with your phone's camera to get vocabulary words related to those objects.

4. Machine Learning-Powered Writing Assistants

Smart Suggestions: Use writing assistants like Grammarly or ProWritingAid that suggest advanced vocabulary words and corrections as you write.

Contextual Learning: These tools can provide explanations and examples of how to use new words in context.

5. Language Exchange VR Platforms

VR Language Exchange: Join VR platforms where you can meet and practice language with native speakers from around the world.

Real-Time Practice: Engage in immersive conversations and cultural exchanges to naturally boost your vocabulary.

6. Gamified Learning Platforms

Gamified Apps: Use apps like Memrise or Duolingo that turn vocabulary learning into an interactive game.

Leaderboards and Challenges: Participate in challenges, earn points, and compete with friends to make learning fun and engaging.

7. Voice-Activated Learning

Smart Speakers: Use smart speakers like Amazon Echo or Google Home to practice new vocabulary by asking for definitions, synonyms, and usage examples.

Interactive Exercises: Engage in voice-based quizzes and games to reinforce learning.

8. Personalized AI Learning Paths

Adaptive Learning: Use AI platforms that adapt to your learning style and pace, providing customized vocabulary lessons based on your progress and preferences.

Progress Tracking: Receive detailed reports on your vocabulary growth and areas that need improvement.

9. Language Learning through Social Media

Hashtag Challenges: Follow language learning hashtags on platforms like Instagram and Twitter to participate in daily vocabulary challenges.

Interactive Content: Engage with posts, stories, and live sessions from language learning influencers and communities.

10. Smartphone Augmented Reality Apps

Language AR Apps: Use AR apps like MondlyAR, which overlay new vocabulary words and phrases onto real-world objects through your smartphone camera.

Interactive Scenes: Explore AR scenes that teach you vocabulary in context, such as virtual grocery stores or travel scenarios.

11. Speech Recognition Tools

Voice Dictation: Practice vocabulary by using speech-to-text features on your smartphone or computer to dictate sentences and passages.

Feedback: Receive immediate feedback on pronunciation and word usage.

12. Virtual Language Learning Clubs

Virtual Meetups: Join virtual language learning clubs where you can practice new vocabulary through discussions, presentations, and collaborative projects.

Peer Learning: Learn and exchange new words with peers in a supportive virtual environment.

13. Customizable Vocabulary Widgets

Widget Apps: Use customizable widget apps on your smartphone to display a new word on your home screen every day.

Interactive Widgets: Tap on the widget for definitions, example sentences, and pronunciation guides.

14. AI-Powered Story Generation

Interactive Stories: Use AI tools to generate stories that incorporate new vocabulary words you want to learn.

Custom Content: Create personalized stories or scenarios to see how new words are used in different contexts.

15. Virtual Reality Field Trips

VR Field Trips: Take virtual field trips to museums, historical sites, or foreign cities using VR platforms.

Contextual Learning: Learn new vocabulary related to the places you visit and the experiences you have in the virtual world.

By leveraging these ultramodern methods, you'll find vocabulary building to be not only effective but also an exciting and immersive experience. Happy learning!

www.ingramcontent.com/pod-product-compliance
Lightning Source LLC
Chambersburg PA
CBHW040906130726
48005CB00019BA/2997